The Great Enterprise from a Reformed Perspective

The Great Enterprise from a Reformed Perspective

Bringing Modern Missions Back to the Bible

J. N. Bolt

WIPF & STOCK · Eugene, Oregon

THE GREAT ENTERPRISE FROM A REFORMED PERSPECTIVE
Bringing Modern Missions Back to the Bible

Copyright © 2012 . All rights reserved. Except for brief quotations in critical publications or reviews, no part of this book may be reproduced in any manner without prior written permission from the publisher. Write: Permissions, Wipf and Stock Publishers, 199 W. 8th Ave., Suite 3, Eugene, OR 97401.

Wipf & Stock
An Imprint of Wipf and Stock Publishers
199 W. 8th Ave., Suite 3
Eugene, OR 97401

www.wipfandstock.com

ISBN 13: 978-1-62032-181-2

Manufactured in the U.S.A.

Unless otherwise indicated, all Scripture quotations are taken from the New American Standard Bible®, Copyright © 1960, 1962, 1963, 1968, 1971, 1972, 1973, 1975, 1977, 1995 by The Lockman Foundation. Used by permission.

Contents

Acknowledgments vii

Introduction ix

1 What Is the Great Enterprise? 1

2 The Eternal Covenant and Election of the Saints as a Help, Not a Hindrance, to the Great Enterprise and the Spread of the Gospel 13

3 The Office of Missionary/Evangelist 25

4 The Missionary Calling and the Setting Apart of the Missionary 36

5 Supporting the Missionary 50

6 Where Is the Missionary to Go? 65

7 The Missionary's Preaching 76

8 The Missionary's Teaching 90

9 The Missionary's Shepherding 109

10 The Missionary and Suffering 123

APPENDIX:
What Is the End for Which God Created the World? 133

Bibliography 143

Acknowledgments

Gratitude must be expressed to Maksim Nelkin for his stalwart friendship and for his living example of the Reformed faith in a missionary context. I would also like to thank the people and leadership of Truth Reformed Bible Church in Golden, Colorado for their sincere fellowship, encouragement in the cause of Christ, and theological instruction. My loving wife deserves the most thanks, not only for her service to this project but also for her willingness and eagerness to follow me around the world for the sake of Christ and the spread of his gospel.

Introduction

THE INGATHERING OF GOD'S elect from among the nations is one of the greatest enterprises of human history, and the church has a central role to play in the endeavor. The gospel will be preached throughout the whole world as a testimony to all the nations (viz., Matt 24:14). Christ will build his whole church, and the gates of hell will not prevail against her (viz., Matt 16:18). The ransomed of God will indeed come from every tribe, tongue, people, and nation (viz., Rev 5:9). Those whom God has chosen, he will ultimately justify and glorify (viz., Rom 8:30). This will happen. God will see to it, and he will see that it happens through the church's missionaries who are sent throughout the world to preach the gospel (viz., Rom 10:15) and teach the nations to obey all that Christ has commanded (viz., Matt 28:20).

The mission of the church, in terms of the ingathering of God's elect from among the nations, is to properly send qualified missionaries to preach the gospel and organize local churches in areas of the world where the gospel has not yet taken root and where the church does not yet exist. However, modern missionary activity has, in many ways, morphed into a philanthropic enterprise to eradicate hunger and other kinds of suffering, while neglecting the preaching of the gospel. This has resulted in unqualified individuals being improperly sent to do good deeds among the nations, which is then called "missions." The aim of this book is to direct the church's attention back to the biblical mandate for missions and missionary activity by outlining the role and office of the missionary and the manner in which the church is to send him.

The focus of this book is quite narrow, examining only the biblical office of missionary as found in Ephesians 4:11 and its relationship to and interaction with the church. This does not mean, however, that there is

Introduction

not a place for lay people in the mission field. A perfect example of lay people serving in the field would be the host of men and women teaching children of missionaries in private Christian schools around the world. These children need an education, and those who teach them provide a great service and are a great help in the cause of the Great Commission. There is a plethora of ways in which lay people can serve the church both at home and abroad as the gospel spreads throughout the world. The aim of this book, though, is to address that which is most neglected by the church today, namely, the sending and supporting of ordained missionaries to preach the gospel and make disciples.

This book serves as a reminder to the church of her responsibility to the world and to her people and introduces the biblical framework within which missionary activity is to take place. When the church fulfills her responsibilities and when missionaries are given the ability and authority to preach the gospel, God's children who are scattered across the face of the earth will respond in faith, and the knowledge of the glory of God will cover the earth as the waters cover the sea (viz., Hab 2:14). When the church neglects her responsibility by sending out untrained individuals who act more like philanthropists than preachers, the nations are left wanting of the gospel and the joy of salvation in Jesus Christ.

In an effort to encourage missionary success and help the church fulfill her role, this book outlines precisely the role for both the church and her missionaries in the ingathering of God's elect from the nations. With both responsibilities clearly defined from Scripture, this book is a significant step forward in reforming modern missionary activity and bringing the mission of the church back to the Bible. May the Lord bless the church through this book and cause his face to shine upon her, that his ways may be known on the earth and his salvation among all nations (viz., Ps 67:1–2).

I also encourage the reader to head Paul's warning in 1 Thessalonians 5:21, where he says to "examine everything carefully; and hold fast to that which is good." Every argument in this book ought to be examined carefully in accordance with the Scriptures. The words of this book must to be taken to heart only inasmuch as they concur with the words of Scripture. I have done my utmost to exposit what I believe the Scriptures principally teach regarding missionary activity, but the reader must examine my words wisely. Scripture is the final authority on all matters pertaining to faith and practice, and I pray that what I have written is a faithful rendition of the Scriptures' teaching. Examine everything; and having done so, hold fast to that which is good.

one

What Is the Great Enterprise?

BEFORE THE FOUNDATION OF the world, God designed what I call the "Great Enterprise." The chief end of this enterprise is the widespread display of the glory of God. This enterprise today is known as the "Great Commission" or "missions." In an effort to bring clarity of meaning to this concept, however, I call it the "Great Enterprise," because the term "missions" is far too vague in the way it is understood. Also, the Great Commission is generally understood as only pertaining to the few New Testament passages where Christ commissioned the apostles to make disciples of all nations. The Great Enterprise, of which the Great Commission is an element, encompasses a far greater scope than Christ's last words prior to his ascension. This enterprise has been in the mind of God from all eternity, has played out through the whole of human history, and will culminate in the ingathering of the last of God's elect to be brought into the kingdom. The purpose of this chapter is to outline what God has revealed concerning the design of this enterprise.

When a designer designs something, he looks at the end or goal that he desires to achieve and then puts together his scheme or strategy that he believes will ultimately lead to the stated goal. Designing the directions to get from one geographic location to another is a simple yet clear and accurate example. If the final destination is unknown, then the directions cannot be determined. Only when the final destination is known can the design even be attempted. Therefore, God's design of the Great Enterprise is intrinsically linked to the chief end or goal of the enterprise; and in order to outline the design, we must first comprehend the chief end.

The Great Enterprise from a Reformed Perspective

Not much time will be devoted here to the nature of the chief end of the Great Enterprise due to the assumption that the reader accepts the fact that God always acts to uphold his own honor and glory and that the display of this glory is what God chiefly aims at in all his works. If this is not accepted, please see the Appendix for a detailed supporting argument derived mostly from Jonathan Edwards's *A Dissertation Concerning the End for Which God Created the World*. In order to avoid confusion, however, let me make clear exactly what I mean by saying that God chiefly aims at the display of his glory in all of his works. The most honorable and glorious being in the universe is God. Therefore, it would be unjust for any being to ascribe more honor and glory to anything other than God. This is true of all beings, whether created or not. For a man to honor something more than God would be idolatry. For God to honor something more than God would also be idolatry. Due to God's perfection, he does not commit idolatry and must always honor and glorify himself more than any other thing. God must, on the basis of his divine character, always act to uphold his honor and display his glory. Therefore, the chief end aimed at in God's Great Enterprise is the upholding of his honor and the display of his glory.

Definition of the Great Enterprise

Before we turn to the design of the upholding of God's honor and display of his glory within the Great Enterprise, let us first define what is meant by the "Great Enterprise." This is God's eternal plan to demonstrate his worth and, thus, his place as the most honorable and glorious being through the ingathering of his elect from among all the tribes, tongues, peoples, and nations of the earth. As for the plan's eternality, we see in 2 Timothy 1:9 that God "saved us and called us with a holy calling, not according to our works, but according to His own purpose and grace which was granted us in Christ Jesus from all eternity." Referring to the Great Enterprise, Paul says that God has saved us and called us according to his purpose. As a result, we received grace in eternity past, which means that the Great Enterprise has been in the mind of God for eternity.

As for the demonstration of God's worth, let us consider Revelation 5:1–9. In this chapter, John says that he saw "in the right hand of Him who sat on the throne a book written inside and on the back, sealed up with seven seals" (v. 1). The problem John encountered was that no one in heaven or on earth or under the earth could be found worthy to open the book and break its seals. Then one of the elders spoke, saying, "Stop weeping; behold, the Lion that is from the tribe of Judah, the Root of David, has overcome so as to open the book and its seven seals" (v. 5). Then the Lamb, standing as if slain, came and took the book. When he had taken the book, the four living creatures and twenty-four elders fell down before the Lamb and sang a new song, saying, "Worthy are you to take the book and to break its seals; for You were slain, and purchased for God with Your blood men from every tribe and tongue and people and nation" (v. 9). That which the four living creatures and the twenty-four elders declared is important to note. First, they declared the worth of the Lamb. Then, they stated the basis of his worth. The Lamb was, and still is, worthy because he was slain and ransomed for God, with his blood, men from every tribe and tongue and people and nation. So, the worth of God is demonstrated through Christ's ransoming of God's elect from among all the peoples of the earth.

The Design of the Enterprise

With the definition stated and rooted firmly in Scripture, let us now move on to the design of the enterprise. Three parts to the enterprise will be addressed. First, the eternal scope of the enterprise will be considered. While the definition of the Great Enterprise touched on this, we will attend to it in much greater detail with an exposition of Ephesians 1:3–6. Second, the enterprise has played out through the whole of human history. We will observe historical accounts of this within the biblical text. Third, the enterprise will culminate when the full number of the saints has been brought into the kingdom of God.

The Scope of the Enterprise

In Ephesians 1:3–6, it is clearly seen that the scope of the Great Enterprise reaches to eternity past. This passage contains the first recorded act of God in history and claims that it happened prior to the foundation of the world. This first act that happened before the foundation of the world was the initial implementation of the Great Enterprise. In verse 3, Paul blesses God the Father on account of his blessing the saints with every spiritual blessing in the heavenly places in Christ. Paul continues in verses 4 to 5 with clear statements as to what those blessings are. God chose the saints in Christ before the creation of the world. This is significant for two reasons. First, God's having chosen the saints before creation places the merit of their having been chosen and the blessings declared in Ephesians 1:3–6 squarely and undeniably with God. Saints have not been chosen or received any blessing on account of anything that they have done or will do. Paul exposits this further in Ephesians 2:8–9, where he says, "For by grace you have been saved through faith; and that not of yourselves, it is the gift of God; not as a result of works, so that no one may boast." God chose the saints before he founded the world so that they would be unable to claim any of his blessings as having come to them on the basis of their own merit. Remember, the chief end of the enterprise is the upholding of God's honor and the display of his glory. Therefore, God's choosing the saints honors and glorifies him, not the saints, because it exemplifies God's work as honorable and glorious.

This idea, which is God's glorious work in contrast to man's inability to work, is exhibited repeatedly in the Scriptures. For the benefit of the reader, a brief list of these examples has been compiled. John 10:26 clearly states man's inability. The Feast of Dedication was taking place in Jerusalem, and Jesus was walking in the temple in the portico of Solomon. The Jews gathered around him and began asking him to tell them plainly whether or not he was the Christ. Jesus responded in John 10:25, saying, "I told you, and you do not believe." He then gave the reason for their unbelief in verse 26, saying, "But you do not believe because you are not of My sheep." The implication is that only those who are of Christ's sheep are able to believe. Those not of Christ's sheep cannot believe, and the only way to be of Christ's sheep is to have been chosen in him prior to the foundation of the world.

A very similar statement is found in John 6:44. Here again, the Jews were grumbling about Jesus because he claimed to be "the bread that came down out of heaven" (John 6:41). Jesus rebuked them for grumbling and said, "No one can come to Me unless the Father who sent Me draws him" (John 6:44). Both God's ability and man's inability are explicitly stated in this verse. No one can come to Christ apart from being drawn by the Father. For a man to come to Christ on his own is an impossibility. The only

What Is the Great Enterprise?

thing that can overcome this impossibility is the ability of God, namely, God's drawing of his elect to himself.

Christ made a similar statement in Matthew 11:27. He was praising God for having hidden these things from the wise and intelligent and claimed that "no one knows the Son except the Father; nor does anyone know the Father except the Son, and anyone to whom the Son wills to reveal Him." Again, man's inability is contrasted with God's ability. There is no one who is able to come to the knowledge of God unless the Son bestows such knowledge upon him. This reality deflects honor and glory from the creature and ascribes it where it is due, namely, to God.

Lastly, God's choosing of his elect is seen to result in the glory of God in Acts 13:48. Paul and Barnabas had been preaching in Pisidian Antioch. On the next Sabbath, nearly the whole city came to the synagogue to hear the word of the Lord. Seeing the crowds, the Jews became jealous and began to blaspheme. As a result, Paul turned and preached to the Gentiles. "When the Gentiles heard this, they began rejoicing and glorifying the word of the Lord; and as many as had been appointed to eternal life believed" (Acts 13:48). The only requirement listed for those that believed is that they were appointed to eternal life. Thus, they believed and began to glorify the word of the Lord. This shows that man is totally helpless apart from God and worthy of nothing, while God is omnipotent and worthy of all honor and glory.

Returning to Ephesians 1:4, the second reason why God's choosing the saints before the foundation of the world is significant is because of its timing. Why did God elect them before the founding of the world? Could God not have simply chosen them before their birth and still demonstrated his glory through the contrast of his ability and their inability? One can argue that the eternal covenant, which secures the saints' election, must have been made prior to the fall of Adam as the federal head of humanity, but this does not address the question of why God purposed it from eternity past. If God chose the saints so that the glory of his grace might be praised as is stated in Ephesians 1:6, why would God do the choosing at a time when nothing existed other than himself? Remember, the display of God's glory is what is aimed at, and this display is infinitely more marvelous than any other kind of display in the universe. If joy for the creature is found in the display of God's glory, how much more, then, is joy for the Creator found in the display of God's glory? With perfect eyes to see the exquisite perfections in the design of his choosing the saints, joy must have abounded within God from all eternity as he chose them in Christ before the foundation of the world. The timing of God's choosing the saints was for the benefit of God, that he might enjoy the display of his own perfection.

Continuing with the blessings recorded in Ephesians 1:4–5, God chose the saints that they would be holy and blameless before him. At first glance, having holy and blameless creatures before God seems to deflect honor and glory from him. How could having holy and blameless saints be a display of God's glory? Is this not rather a display of the glory of the saints? On the contrary, it is not a display of the glory of the saints but instead a display of the glory of God. Paul explains this concept in Ephesians 5:26–27. Paul draws an analogy between husband and wife and Christ and the church, and he says that Christ loved the church and gave himself up for her "so that He might sanctify her . . . that He might present to Himself the church in all her glory, having no spot or wrinkle or any such thing; but that she would be holy and blameless." The last phrase is a link back to Ephesians 1:4. Saints were chosen to be holy and blameless in Ephesians 1:4, and Ephesians 5:27 states that Christ will present the church to himself as holy and blameless. There is a pertinent question that must be asked. Namely, why does Christ present the church to himself? Does he do so in order to observe her inherent beauty? There is no inherent beauty in the church. So, where does the beauty come from? Verses 25 to 26 of Ephesians 5 give the answer. Christ gave himself up for the church in order that he might sanctify her and cleanse her. She is inherently evil and filthy, but the work of Christ cleanses and purifies her so that she might be presented in all her glory. The glory that she then has is the display of what Christ has done in her and is, thus, a reflection of his own glory. Therefore, Christ presents the church to himself in all her glory so that he might observe his own handiwork in the sanctification and cleansing of his bride.

There is yet another blessing that Paul addresses. In Ephesians 1:5, Paul says that God "predestined us to adoption as sons through Jesus Christ to Himself, according to the kind intention of His will." Shown again here is that the intention of God's sovereign will is the basis of the blessing. Saints have not been adopted because God saw them as a positive addition to the family. Rather, they have been adopted according to the intention of God's will. What is the intention of God's will? Already known is that he intends to uphold his honor and display his glory. So, what does the adoption of the saints have to do with God's honor and glory? Peter answers this question in 1 Peter 2:9, saying, "But you are a chosen race, a royal priesthood, a holy nation, a people for God's own possession, so that you may proclaim the excellencies of Him who has called you out of darkness into His marvelous light." That the saints are for God's own possession is a clear reference to their adoption as sons, and they have been adopted so that they may proclaim God's excellencies. In other words, God has adopted the saints and taken possession of them so that they may declare the manifold perfection of God.

There is yet one more brief but important point in Ephesians 1 that must be considered. Verse 6 presents the purpose for which God has blessed the saints with every spiritual blessing in the heavenly places. God has done it all "to the praise of the glory of His grace" (Eph 1:6). This is an explicit statement that God has acted from eternity past to ransom his elect, with the ultimate goal of the glory of his grace being praised.

The Enterprise Exhibited throughout Human History

There are many examples in history where the Great Enterprise has been exhibited. Thus, the focus will now turn to one of those examples in order to place the Great Commission squarely within the Great Enterprise. The example is found in Acts 1:1–8, a passage that is accurately understood as Christ's commissioning of his apostles just prior to his ascension to be his witnesses to the remotest part of the earth. Similar words are recorded at the end of all three Synoptic Gospels. The summary of all four accounts is a commissioning of the apostles to go throughout the entire world as Christ's witnesses and preach the gospel to all the various peoples of the earth, teaching them to obey all that Christ has commanded. While there is interpretive disagreement as to what it means to make disciples and to what extent this commission applies to anyone beyond the apostles, the immediate meaning of Christ's commissioning the apostles to preach the gospel is widely accepted.

Where the inaccuracies arise in Acts 1:1–8 is in the relationship between the apostles' question in verse 6 and Christ's answer in verses 7 to 8. The commonly accepted interpretation is that the disciples asked a question, out of context, in verse 6 regarding the restoration of the kingdom to Israel. Christ then brushed aside their question in verse 7, changed the subject in verse 8, and then commissioned the apostles. However, this is an inaccurate reading of the text.

The disciples knew exactly what they were asking. What Luke, the author of Acts, says in verse 3 is important. Christ presented himself to the apostles after his suffering for a period of forty days, speaking of matters concerning the kingdom of God. Luke chose to summarize everything that Christ spoke for forty days as "concerning the kingdom of God" (Acts 1:3). Undoubtedly, Christ spoke about other matters during that time, but it is significant that Luke chose to summarize all of it by saying that Christ spoke to them things concerning the kingdom of God.

Acts 1:4–8 then gives one specific account of what Christ spoke. Christ gathered the disciples together and commanded them not to leave Jerusalem but instead to wait for the Holy Spirit. In response, the disciples asked a question in verse 6, saying, "Lord, is it at this time You are restoring the kingdom to Israel?" This was a natural question to ask, as Christ had been speaking to them concerning the kingdom of God over a period of forty days and then told them to wait in Jerusalem for that which the Father had promised. Though they were still looking for the restoration of a physical kingdom, their question about the timing of the restoration of the kingdom was not out of context; and Christ answered their question, starting in verse 7 and continuing through verse 8. He said very simply that it was not for them to know the times or epochs but that they would receive power from the Holy Spirit and would be Christ's witnesses in Jerusalem, Judea, Samaria, and even to the most remote parts of the earth. With this answer, Christ lodged the Great Commission squarely inside God's enterprise to gather into his kingdom all of his elect from among all the peoples of the earth.

The language of this passage is strikingly similar to that of an early manifestation of the Great Enterprise found in Genesis 12:1–3, which contains the promises of the Abrahamic covenant. "Now the LORD said to Abram, 'Go forth from your country, And from your relatives And from your father's house, To the land which I will show you; And I will make you a great nation, And I will bless you, And make your name great; And so you shall be a blessing; And I will bless those who bless you, And the one who curses you I will curse. And in you all the families of the earth will be blessed.'" The first promise here is that God shall make Abraham a great nation, and included in this promise is that this nation will have a land in which to dwell. "Go forth . . . To the land which I will show you" (v. 1). This promise does not say that Abraham himself will become a great nation but rather that his descendants after him will be a great and numerous people. This is explained further in Genesis 26:3b–4a, where God spoke to Isaac, saying, "I will establish the oath which I swore to your father Abraham. I will multiply your descendants as the stars of heaven, and will give your descendants all these lands." Here, God explained that it is through Abraham's descendants that God will establish the oath he made to Abraham. So, God will give Abraham numerous descendants that will be a great nation and inhabit a specific land. This is the first promise. The next promise is that God will bless Abraham and make his name great. This is not two promises but only one because it is the blessing of Abraham that causes his name to be great. An important question is then raised. What does it mean for God to bless Abraham? This question will be addressed shortly. For now, the examination of the promises continues.

Next, God said, "And so you shall be a blessing" (v. 2). The word "so" indicates a means by which something takes place. In other words, whatever happened prior to this statement is the means by which Abraham shall be a blessing. Therefore, Abraham shall be a blessing as a result of his having numerous descendants who will be a great nation and inhabit a specific land, and of his being blessed and having a great name. In order to understand what is going on here, it is imperative to understand the answer to the question that was previously raised. Namely, what is a blessing? Abraham will be blessed, and in that way he will be a blessing. What is the text referring to regarding a blessing?

The answer was hinted at previously in Ephesians 1. God's first work that is recorded in Ephesians 1:3–6 sheds light on the issue. Ephesians 1 says that God has blessed his saints just as he chose them, predestined them, freely bestowed grace upon them, redeemed them, forgave them, made known the mystery of his will to them, and gave them an inheritance. In other words, God's choosing them, predestining them, freely bestowing grace upon them, redeeming them, forgiving them, making known the mystery of his will to them, and giving them an inheritance—all to the end of the praise of the glory of his grace—is his blessing of them. The blessing of God is, therefore, his predestining, calling, justifying, and ultimately glorifying his saints (viz., Rom 8:29–30) as a display of his glory.

The Great Enterprise from a Reformed Perspective

In Genesis 12, it is now clear that God's blessing of Abraham is God's display of his glory through not only Abraham but also through his descendants by predestining, calling, justifying, and ultimately glorifying them. Furthermore, it is through this blessing that Abraham and his descendants who follow him are a blessing. One question still remains—namely, to whom are Abraham and his descendants a blessing? The last promise in the covenant gives the answer. "And in you all the families of the earth will be blessed" (v. 3). All the families of the earth will receive the blessing of God's predestining, calling, justifying, and ultimately glorifying them as the display of his glory.

This was the greatest and furthest reaching promise in the covenant that sat at the foundation of the Old Testament's teaching concerning the kingdom of God. While the full extent of the promise may not have been in the minds of the disciples when they posed their question to Jesus, it certainly was in his mind when he gave them the answer. "'Lord, is it at this time You are restoring the kingdom to Israel?' He said to them, 'It is not for you to know times or epochs which the Father has fixed by His own authority; but you will receive power when the Holy Spirit has come upon you; and you shall be My witnesses both in Jerusalem, and in all Judea and Samaria, and even to the remotest part of the earth'" (Acts 1:6b–8). The disciples were asking about the timing of the fulfillment of the oath made to Abraham, and Jesus responded by telling them exactly what God told Abraham in Genesis 12:3. There is an important correlation between these two passages: "And in you all the families of the earth will be blessed" (Gen 12:3), and "You shall be my witnesses . . . to the remotest part of the earth" (Acts 1:8). The correlation is even clearer in the way Christ is quoted in Luke's gospel. "Thus it is written, that the Christ would suffer and rise again from the dead the third day, and that repentance for forgiveness of sins would be proclaimed in His name to all the nations, beginning from Jerusalem" (Luke 24:46–47). The descendants of Abraham shall preach the gospel among all nations and families, even in the remotest part of the earth. This is the fulfillment of God's oath to Abraham and the restoration of the kingdom of God, all with a view to God's people praising his glory as displayed through the fulfillment of God's oath to Abraham and the ingathering of God's elect from among all the nations.

One final passage will now be considered in order to solidify the claim that the Great Enterprise has been manifested throughout human

What Is the Great Enterprise?

history. This passage, Isaiah 52, is chosen because it is the basis of Paul's ambition to fulfill his role within the Great Enterprise, which is found in Romans 15:19–21. This passage in Romans will be looked at in greater detail in chapter 4, when the missionary's inward calling is addressed. For now, let the following be considered. In Romans 15:19, Paul says that he has fully preached the gospel from Jerusalem all the way around to Illyricum. Thus in verse 20, Paul says that it is his ambition to preach the gospel where the name of Christ has not yet been proclaimed. Verse 21 states the reason behind this ambition.

Remember, this is the same Paul who was met by the risen Christ on the road to Damascus and commissioned as an apostle. Jesus is quoted in Acts 9:15 as saying, "[Paul] is a chosen instrument of Mine, to bear My name before the Gentiles and kings and the sons of Israel." This seems to be a fairly good reason for Paul's ambition for missionary service. Why would Paul want to preach the gospel where Christ had not yet been named? The expected answer would be that Paul was chosen by Christ as his instrument to bear Christ's name before the Gentiles. Amazingly, this is not how Paul answers the question.

Paul answers by quoting Isaiah 52:15b, which says, "For what had not been told them they will see, And what they had not heard they will understand." Verses 13 to 15 of Isaiah 52 are a prophecy of the exaltation of Christ. "Behold, My servant will prosper, He will be high and lifted up and greatly exalted" (v. 13). Every reference in the Gospels to Christ being lifted up is a reference to his being lifted up on the cross and crucified. Isaiah 52:14 supports this by referencing his "marred" appearance. "Just as many were astonished at you, My people, So His appearance was marred more than any man And His form more than the sons of men." Verse 15a speaks of Christ's atoning for the peoples and of those in authority being astonished at him. "Thus He will sprinkle many nations, Kings will shut their mouths on account of Him." Then, in verse 15b, are the lines quoted by Paul as the foundation of his ambition to preach Christ among those who have not yet heard. "For what had not been told them they will see, And what they had not heard they will understand." What had not been told them, and what had they not heard? "Break forth, shout joyfully together, You waste places of Jerusalem; For the Lord has comforted His people, He has redeemed Jerusalem. The Lord has bared His holy arm In the sight of all the nations, That all the ends of the earth may see The salvation of our God" (Isa 52:9–10).

The Great Enterprise from a Reformed Perspective

The Great Enterprise is seen throughout human history. It is the furthest reaching promise of the Abrahamic covenant in Genesis 12:3. The Great Enterprise is recorded in the prophesies of Isaiah. Nearly all of the apostles were killed while working towards the ingathering of God's elect from among the nations, and Paul's ambition in life was to extend the gospel to all the nations.

The Culmination of the Enterprise

The Great Enterprise will culminate in the ingathering of the last of God's elect into the kingdom of God. This is implied in Mark 13:10, where Christ is quoted as saying, "The gospel must first be preached to all the nations." This statement is expanded in Matthew 24:14. The disciples came to Christ and asked about the timing of the destruction of the temple. He answered their question and more, saying, "This gospel of the kingdom shall be preached in the whole world as a testimony to all the nations, and then the end will come." So, the end will come when the gospel is preached and testimony given to all nations. This is also clear in 2 Thessalonians 1:10, which states that Christ will come in the end "to be glorified in His saints on that day, and to be marveled at among all who have believed." When Christ returns, he will return to be marveled at among all who have believed. He will not return to be marveled at among some of his saints. He will only return when he can be in the midst of all his saints. His return will be the culmination of the Great Enterprise. Since his return will be to all, not some, of his saints, and will come once the gospel is preached as a testimony to all the nations, the culmination of the Great Enterprise will be at the ingathering of God's final elect from among the nations into the kingdom of God.

two

The Eternal Covenant and Election of the Saints as a Help, Not a Hindrance, to the Great Enterprise and the Spread of the Gospel

To say that the doctrine of election only hinders the cause of the Great Enterprise is nothing more than an admission of ignorance. If God has already determined who will go to heaven and who will not, then some argue that there is no point in evangelizing and preaching the gospel. I call this ignorance, because it completely ignores or fails to recognize the fact that people go to heaven by getting saved and that people get saved by calling on the name of the Lord. They call on the name of the Lord only when they believe. They only believe when they hear of whom they are to believe in, and they only hear when someone preaches. Preachers only preach when they are sent (viz., Rom 10:14–15). Thus, it is written, "How beautiful are the feet of those who bring good news of good things!" (Rom 10:15b) In God's determining who would come to faith, he also determined that they would do so through the preaching of the gospel. Without hearing the gospel, it is impossible for a person to be saved. The rest of this chapter shows how the Reformed doctrine of election secures success for the missionary and encourages further missionary activity on the part of the minister of God's word.

The Eternal Covenant

In order to avoid trite caviling about election and the notion of free will, we will first look not to the doctrine of election but to the doctrine in which election is rooted—namely, the doctrine of the eternal covenant or the covenant of grace. By "eternal covenant," I mean that covenant made within the Godhead in eternity past, in which the Father agreed to give certain people, the elect, to the Son, and the Son agreed to act as the elect's representative both on the cross and in the fulfillment of the law. The most common argument against this doctrine is that it is not spelled out precisely in any one passage of Scripture. This, however, does not mean that Scripture does not describe the various aspects of the covenant in various passages. The same is true of the doctrine of the Trinity. No single verse or passage fully explains the doctrine of the Trinity, yet it is a tenet of orthodox Christianity.

That there was an agreement made between God the Father and Christ the Mediator is made clear by Paul in Galatians 3, where he writes about the relationship between the law and God's covenanted promises. Paul says in verse 16 that the promises were made to Abraham and his seed. He then argues that the "seed" was a reference to Jesus Christ, meaning, that God covenanted with Christ and made promises to him. This is a clear indication that there was an agreement between God the Father and Christ the Mediator. Let us now look to the facets of the eternal covenant as found elsewhere in Scripture.

The Father covenanted with or agreed with the Mediator, Christ, that he should be the federal head of his people. That Christ indeed acted as the federal head of his people is seen clearly in Romans 5, where Christ is compared to Adam. Just as through one man, Adam, sin entered the world, so through the one, Jesus Christ, do the many receive the abundance of grace and the gift of righteousness (viz., Rom 5:12–17). Just as Adam acted as the federal head of all his posterity in the garden of Eden, resulting in death and condemnation spreading to all humanity, so Christ has acted as the federal head of all his posterity, resulting in justification and life to the many. Paul intimates the same thing in 1 Corinthians 15:45, where he says, "So also it is written, 'The first man, Adam, became a living soul.' The last Adam became a life-giving spirit." Paul refers to Christ as the "last Adam," meaning, that Christ acted as the federal head of all his posterity in the same way in which Adam had acted previously. That Christ is the head of all his posterity is also clearly seen in Ephesians 5:23, which says that Christ "is the head of the church."

With the reality of an agreement within the Godhead firmly established, let us look to the requirements set forth by the Father in regards to the Mediator. First, the Father required that Christ atone for the sins of those whom the Father had given to him. This is clearly seen in John 6:39 and 10:11–15. Christ was to lay down his life for his sheep, which were to be those who the Father had given to him. Second, Christ was to accomplish that which the first Adam failed to accomplish—namely, the fulfillment of the law, resulting in imputed justification for all of his sheep. This is seen clearly in Galatians 4:4–5. Acting as the federal head of the church, Christ lived perfectly under the law, thus securing justification, and suffered the wrath of God on the cross, thus securing redemption.

In order to act as the "second Adam," Christ had to take on human form, as seen in John 1:14 and Philippians 2:6–9. As a man, Christ had to live under the law, as shown in Galatians 4:4–5. With his work completed, Christ had to apply the secured redemption and justification to his elect. "For as in Adam all die, so also in Christ all will be made alive" (1 Cor 15:22). The entirety of this work is found in Romans 8:29–30. "For those whom He foreknew, He also predestined to be conformed to the image of His Son, so that He would be the firstborn among many brethren; and these whom He predestined, He also called; and these whom He called, He also justified; and these whom He justified, He also glorified." This is where the eternal covenant becomes significant to the Great Enterprise. Christ acted as the federal head and secured all these things for a specific group of people—the elect.

That the elect were chosen and the terms of the covenant agreed upon before the founding of the world is made explicit in Revelation 13:8. John, telling of a book in which names have been written from before the founding of the world, states that those whose names were not written in the book would worship the beast. Those whose names were written in the book would not worship the beast, and this was determined before creation. This is a reference to the election of the saints. As for the terms agreed upon in the eternal covenant, this is seen in the name of the book, which is called "The Book of Life of the Lamb Who Has Been Slain." Written before time began, the book's title references the Lamb that was slain. Therefore, it must have been agreed upon prior to the foundation of the world that the Lamb was to be slain. The eternal covenant was made within the Godhead before time began. As part of the agreement, the Father was to give specific people to the Son, and the Son was to fulfill the law and suffer the wrath of God on their behalf.

Guaranteed Success

Far from discouraging missionary activity, the doctrine of election promises missionary success. Advancing the gospel is not dependent upon the disposition of the hearers or on the eloquence of the preachers. Rather, the only condition is that those who have been appointed to eternal life actually hear the gospel preached. Luke's commentary on the situation in Pisidian Antioch, found in Acts 13, makes this clear. After the Jews became jealous and began to blaspheme, Paul turned and preached to the Gentiles. Luke's commentary is found in verse 48, which says, "When the Gentiles heard this, they began rejoicing and glorifying the word of the Lord; and as many as had been appointed to eternal life believed." The only requirement that Luke lists for their belief is that they had been appointed to eternal life.

The missionary finds further encouragement in Revelation 5:9–10. As noted in the previous chapter, Christ was declared worthy because he has purchased for God, with his blood, men from every tribe and tongue and people and nation. Furthermore, Christ made them to be a kingdom and priests to God. The tense of the verbs must be noted. Christ *has purchased* these men. He *has made* them to be a kingdom and priests. Thus, the work is already done, as men from every tribe and tongue and people and nation have been purchased for God by the blood of Christ. The elect of God already exist. The missionary does not have to somehow convince reprobate men to become children of God. The missionary only has to locate the children of God and proclaim to them the good news of the gospel.

This reality is analogous to a father whose children are lost in the woods. The father recruits everyone who is able to search day and night for his lost children. The only instruction that he gives is to tell everyone who is found the way back to his house. The searchers ask how they will know if someone they might find is one of his children. The father responds, saying, "You will know they are my children when they respond with joy and come home." Anyone not belonging to the father will not care about the way back to his house, yet those belonging to the father will exult at the news as if their lives have been saved.

When the doctrine of election is removed, the analogy becomes one in which the father loses his children in the woods and recruits everyone who is able to search day and night for them. The searchers ask how they will know if someone they might find is one of his children. He responds, saying, "I am not sure who my children are. Anyone you find could be one of them. Therefore, try to convince everyone you find that I am his father and that he should come to my home." Not knowing who his children are, the father is left waiting and hoping that someone somewhere will decide to join his household.

Of the two analogies, only one is accurate, and only one is a help to the cause of the Great Enterprise. God's children are scattered abroad over the face of the whole earth. Christ has purchased men from every tribe and tongue and people and nation on the planet. They are out there, and they will respond with joy and come home upon hearing the good news of the gospel. This indisputable fact should spur bold missionary ventures to the most remote parts of the earth. All that is required of the missionary is to preach the gospel and then teach those who respond in faith to obey all that Christ has commanded. Yes, to preach the gospel is a requirement, for no one can come to saving faith without hearing the good news of the gospel. To this requirement, we now turn.

The Gospel Must Be Preached

Those who criticize the doctrine of election on the basis that it hinders the Great Enterprise ultimately ask and answer incorrectly the question of whether or not a person must hear the gospel in order to be saved. Their argument against election is that if God has already determined that certain people will go to heaven, then there is no need to go throughout the world preaching the gospel. Inherent in this assertion is that hearing the gospel is not a necessary precursor to saving faith. On the contrary, it is precisely because God has determined that certain people will go to heaven that the gospel must be preached throughout the world, for there are none who will come to saving faith without the gospel.

Romans 1:16 says that the gospel "is the power of God for salvation to everyone who believes." The good news of redemption and justification in Jesus Christ is the power of God for salvation. What this verse says is significant. The gospel message itself is God's power for salvation. The power for salvation is found in nothing other than the gospel. Paul expands this argument in Romans 10, saying that salvation comes to "whoever will call on the name of the Lord" (v. 13). He then lays out his argument for the necessity of the gospel, saying in verses 14 to 15, "How then will they call on Him in whom they have not believed? How will they believe in Him whom they have not heard? And how will they hear without a preacher? How will they preach unless they are sent? Just as it is written, 'How beautiful are the feet of those who bring good news of good things!'" Paul's point is that a person must call upon the name of the Lord in order to be saved, and the only way a person can call upon the name of the Lord is if the gospel is preached and heard. Paul's coup de grâce appears in verse 17, which says, "So faith comes by hearing, and hearing by the word of Christ." In other words, saving faith comes by hearing, and hearing comes by the word of Christ. Another way to say it would be that the word of Christ causes hearing, which brings about faith, which leads to salvation.

The conclusion is that one must hear the gospel in order to be saved. There is no salvation outside of faith that has Jesus Christ as its object, and it is impossible to have Jesus Christ as the object of faith without hearing of him as preached in the gospel. The preaching of the gospel is a necessary component of the Great Enterprise. Those who hear the gospel and respond in faith will be welcomed into the kingdom of God. Those who hear the gospel and reject it will be thrown into hell along with all those who never heard the gospel.

Arguments against the Necessity of the Gospel

There are some arguments against this position, namely, that it would unfairly exclude two groups of people from the prospect of salvation. The first group is made up of those spread throughout the world who never hear the gospel. This is the great majority of people throughout human history. Prior to the advent of Christ, God's specific revelation was almost exclusively confined to the nation of Israel. This nation being "the fewest [in number] of all the peoples" (Deut 7:7), the rest of humanity would have been excluded from the possibility of salvation through no fault of their own. They never rejected the gospel, because they had never heard it. On account of God being fair and just, he would never condemn the majority of the human race to hell simply because they had never heard the gospel.

The Eternal Covenant and Election of the Saints

Since the advent of Christ, the gospel has spread throughout all the regions of the world, but a surprisingly large number of individuals still live within groups of people who are isolated from the gospel and are considered to be unreached. According to Joshua Project, a research initiative seeking to highlight the ethnic people groups with the least followers of Jesus Christ, 41.6 percent of the world's population has yet to be reached with the gospel as of 2012.[1] This means that if hearing the gospel is necessary for salvation, then nearly half of the world is already doomed, without any hope of avoiding the wrath of God. This, some argue, would be contrary to the God who so loved the world that he gave himself up for it.

The second group is made up of those with access to some of God's specific revelation but without a clear presentation of the gospel, namely, the Old Testament saints. If, in order to be saved, a person must hear the good news of redemption and justification through the sacrifice of Christ on the cross, then all of the saints who lived prior to the advent of Christ would be excluded from salvation. Scripture clearly teaches that the Old Testament saints are not excluded from salvation (viz., Matt 17:3). Based upon this, some argue that salvation must be possible apart from the hearing of the gospel.

These are fine objections that deserve a legitimate answer. The first objection is that God would not condemn anyone to hell simply because he has not heard the gospel. Indeed, this is true. No one is condemned for the unfortunate reality of never having heard the gospel. Furthermore, no one is condemned for having heard the gospel and rejecting it. Rather, condemnation comes entirely apart from the gospel. For, as Christ said in John 3:18, he who does not believe has been judged already. No one will suffer the wrath of God on the basis of having never heard or having rejected the gospel. Rather, there are two other realities that bring humanity under condemnation; both of which are sufficient to warrant the eternal wrath of God.

The first reality is that all are guilty in Adam. As mentioned earlier in the chapter, there is universal condemnation in Adam, thus bringing all of humanity under the wrath of God. Paul makes this abundantly clear in Romans 5, where he argues that even those who died without the law and those who never sinned in the likeness of Adam still had Adam's guilt imputed to them. It is, therefore, irrelevant whether a person hears the

---

1. "Great Commission Statistics," Joshua Project, line 3.

gospel or not. Everyone deserves the wrath of God on the basis that all sinned in Adam (viz., Rom 5:12).

The second reality is that all have sinned and fallen short of the glory of God (viz., Rom 3:23). The word "fallen short," translated from the original Greek, literally means "to lack." Every human being has sinned against God and lacks his glory. There is no innocent person on an island somewhere who is being treated unfairly by being isolated from the message of the gospel. All people deserve the just wrath of God, for judgment comes not based upon whether or not the gospel is accepted but rather upon the works done in the flesh (viz., Rev 20:13).

No one is unfairly excluded from salvation simply because he never hears the gospel. Rather, people are fairly excluded from salvation due to their sin and rebellion against God. All are guilty; and the only means of deliverance is the message of the gospel of Jesus Christ, which shall be preached throughout the whole world as a testimony to the nations (viz., Matt 24:14).

As for the second objection, it too deserves an appropriate answer. The argument is that making the hearing of the gospel necessary for salvation would exclude the Old Testament saints from salvation. The presupposition in the argument is that the Old Testament saints were somehow excluded from the gospel. This inaccurate view is due mostly to the teaching that a radical discontinuity exists between the testaments, which is widely accepted in evangelical circles today. Believing that the means of salvation was somehow different between the Old Testament and the New Testament, some argue that salvation was possible in the Old Testament apart from the gospel, and may now, therefore, be possible outside of the gospel.

Where they go wrong, though, is in thinking that the means of salvation somehow differs between the testaments. There is only one means of salvation, and that is through the redemption and justification secured by Christ on the cross and applied to the saints through faith. Faith with Christ as its object has always been and will remain the only means of salvation. No one has ever been saved by the law. No one has ever been saved by the sacrifices of animals (viz., Heb 10). Only through the blood of the Lamb of God are atonement and forgiveness possible. This is clearly seen in the faith of Abraham, the father of the nation of Israel. Hebrews makes clear in chapter 11 that Abraham, along with the other patriarchs, was a man of faith. "By faith Abraham, when he was tested, offered up Isaac"

(Heb 11:17a). In what way was Abraham's offering up of Isaac a testimony of his faith? The account is found in Genesis 22, and what it contains will end the argument with the undeniable conclusion that Abraham had the Lamb of God as the object of his faith.

Picking up the story in Genesis 22:1-2, "Now it came about after these things, that God tested Abraham, and said to him, 'Abraham!' And he said, 'Here I am.' He said, 'Take now your son, your only son, whom you love, Isaac, and go to the land of Moriah, and offer him there as a burnt offering on one of the mountains of which I will tell you.'" What happened next was quite astonishing. Abraham rose, possibly the next morning, and headed off with his son, two of his young men, and all of the material necessary for the burnt offering. Verse 4 says that on the third day, Abraham lifted up his eyes and saw the place from a distance. This means that they traveled for three days before even seeing the place to which they were going. For three days, Abraham walked with his son and all of the material for a burnt offering. One has to assume that Abraham and Isaac conversed during this three-day journey. What seems odd, though, is that the text says nothing of those three days. The biblical account goes directly from Abraham's saddling the donkey to his seeing the place on the third day. The text does not explicitly say anything about those three days, but it does say something implicitly about them.

Verse 7 says that as they walked on to the place of the offering, Isaac spoke to his father, saying, "Behold, the fire and the wood, but where is the lamb for the burnt offering?" This indicates that Isaac knew there was to be a burnt offering. Verse 9 says that as they came to the place, Abraham "bound his son Isaac and laid him on the altar." Abraham was at least one hundred years old at this time, and Isaac was roughly twenty years old. Apparently, though, Isaac did not resist or question at all. He simply allowed his father to bind him on the altar. This indicates that Isaac knew that he was to be a burnt offering.

The three-day journey must now be considered. When Abraham arose in the morning and went to get Isaac, surely he asked his father why they were getting up so early and where they were going. Abraham could have responded two different ways, but the text is not clear. He could have responded, "It does not matter. Just do as I say." Isaac probably would have been obedient at that point, but would he have remained obedient all the way to the altar? Conversely, Abraham could have responded, "Son, our Father in heaven has required something of us. Let us go now, and I will make the Lord's will plain to you." Isaac would have surely been obedient, and he would have obediently climbed onto the altar after three days of his father explaining what God had requested of them.

What else would they have talked about for three days? For any father on that journey with his son, small talk would not have been an option. Any father's goal during that journey ought to have been to clearly and precisely explain the person and purposes of God to his son. Isaac was to die, and Abraham had three days left with his son. Any father with only three days left with his son would spend every moment teaching him who God is and the intricacies of his eternal plan of redemption.

Further insight into the whole of the situation is found in Isaac's question in verse 7 regarding the lamb for the burnt offering and Abraham's answer in verse 8. If Isaac was expecting to be the burnt offering, why did he ask about the lamb? Furthermore, if Abraham expected to slay Isaac (viz., Heb 11:19), why did he tell Isaac that "God will provide for Himself the lamb for the burnt offering" in verse 8?

In the three days that Abraham spent explaining the person and purposes of God, he undoubtedly spoke to Isaac of the human condition. The fact is that everyone, including Isaac, deserves to die, for all of have fallen short and exchanged the glory of God for the glory of created images (viz., Rom 1:23). God could at any moment smite all of humanity, and he would do no one any wrong. It is only by grace that men are given each additional breath. Now, the time had come for Isaac's last breath, and it was to come at the hand of his father. Therefore, seeing the wood and the fire that was to consume him, Isaac asked, "Where is the lamb that is to atone for my God-hating wickedness? I am about to die and meet him face to face. Physical death does not frighten me, but suffering the eternal wrath of God is beyond terrifying. Father, where is the lamb for the burnt offering?"

Still expecting to slay his son, Abraham replied, "God will provide for Himself the lamb for the burnt offering," my son (v. 8). Then, the two of them walked on together to complete that which God had requested of them. So, Abraham believed that God would provide for himself a lamb, but he still intended to slay his son. Why would Abraham still intend to slay his son if he expected God to provide a lamb? That which Abraham expected God to provide was not a lamb to be slain on that altar on that day. The Lamb that he expected was to be slain later at Calvary to atone for the sins of not only Abraham and Isaac but also for the children of God scattered abroad (viz., John 11:51–52).

The mercy displayed in verse 12 was magnificent. Abraham stretched out his hand to slay his son, and the Angel of the Lord stopped him. Oh, what a joyous moment that surely was. By grace, the Lord extended to Isaac another breath. In response, Abraham and Isaac worshiped God. Seeing a ram caught in the thicket by its horns, Abraham took it and offered it in the place where his son had been, and Abraham called the name of the place "The Lord Will Provide."

This ram, however, was not the lamb that God would provide for himself. Of note, first, is that it was a ram and not a lamb. Second, the text says nothing of the ram being supplied by God. Yes, God did supply the ram in the sense that he is the provider of all things, but the text only says that the ram was caught in the thicket. It could have been, and probably was, there the entire time. Third, the name that Abraham gave the place is significant. He called it "The Lord Will Provide." This name indicates the future tense. He did not name the place "The Lord Has Provided." Abraham was still expecting the Lord to provide for himself a Lamb.

In an incredible display of grace and mercy, God spared the life of Isaac. In response, Abraham and Isaac worshiped God on the mountain and offered up a ram. With expectant hope, both of them waited upon God to provide for himself a Lamb that would atone for their sin. Their faith was that "in the mount of the Lord it will be provided" (v. 14b). That which the Lord would provide was he who "was pierced through for our transgressions, He was crushed for our iniquities; The chastening for our well-being fell upon Him, And by His scourging we are healed" (Isa 53:5). Abraham placed his faith in the Lamb that God would provide. Isaiah makes clear that he, "Like a lamb that is led to slaughter" (Isa 53:7), rendered himself as a guilt offering (viz., Isa 53:10); and upon seeing Jesus, John the Baptist declared in John 1:29, "Behold, the Lamb of God who takes away the sin of the world!"

The undeniable conclusion is that Abraham's saving faith was in Christ the Mediator. The redemption and justification that Abraham waited and hoped for was the redemption and justification that Christ has secured for his elect through his life, death, and resurrection. The means of salvation has always been the same. The law and the prophets have testified of and pointed to Christ (viz., John 5:39), and their message has always been and will always be the power of God for salvation and a necessary precursor to saving faith.

Conclusion

So, it is true that making the hearing of the gospel necessary for salvation excludes a great majority of men presently and throughout history from the prospect of salvation. This, however, is not unfair, for all deserve the just wrath of God. There is no one who will be unjustly condemned, and it is an amazing expression of mercy on God's part that he continues to delay his wrath in order to display his mercy upon his elect and patiently bring all of them to repentance (viz., Rom 9:22–23; 2 Pet 3:7–9). Furthermore, no saint is somehow kept from salvation simply because he lived prior to the advent of Christ. All of God's specific revelation has testified concerning God's eternal plan of redemption, and all saving faith has always had the Lamb of God as its object.

God the Father made a covenant with Christ the Mediator before the foundation of the world, in which it was agreed upon that Christ would come to earth as a man and redeem the children of God through Christ's obedience to the law and sacrificial death on the cross. Christ has purchased specific individuals from every tribe and tongue and people and nation, whose names were written down in a book before time began. He will not lose any of them (viz., John 6:39). They will hear the call, and they will come (viz., Rom 8:29–30).

This reality does not hinder the cause of the Great Enterprise or the spread of the gospel. Rather, it spurs both in that it guarantees success for the missionary and compels the minister of God's word to extend the preaching of the gospel. The elect of God will respond to the gospel in faith. When the Father's lost children learn the way home, they will rejoice and come running. Because of God's compassion, ministers of God's word must search the woods day and night for his lost children, for the children of God must be told of the way home.

three

The Office of Missionary/Evangelist

OF PRIMARY IMPORTANCE IN the Great Enterprise is the church office of missionary/evangelist. This is the office that actually executes the church's work within the Great Enterprise; yet, surprisingly, it is often neglected and widely misunderstood. Like many biblical teachings, the concept of the missionary office is not explicitly laid out in Scripture; and rather than looking for the hidden diamonds in the rough of the Bible's pages, too many people throughout modern history have simply speculated or used the natural studies like psychology and anthropology to determine who a missionary is and what he does. This should not be so. The church should look to the Bible as not *a rule* but rather *the rule* for faith and practice. To the Bible we now turn to examine the issue of who a missionary is and what he does.

The Church Office

One can go to ten different churches and ask a pastor or elder from each church to define the missionary role, and he will end up with ten different answers. At times, even elders from the same congregation will provide differing definitions. Assuming these are biblical churches, this is not the case when the question pertains to the role of the pastor. There may be some varied nuances, but there is widespread agreement within orthodox Christianity that the role of the pastor is to shepherd the flock through the teaching and prescribing of doctrine and to act judiciously in matters of disagreement and discipline. With the evangelist listed alongside the pastor in Ephesians 4:11, there should be a common understanding regarding both roles. The office of evangelist itself, however, is commonly neglected and/or rejected, thus leading to widespread confusion as to who the evangelist is and what he does.

The offices of the church are found in Ephesians 4:11–12, which says, "And He gave some as apostles, and some as prophets, and some as evangelists, and some as pastors and teachers, for the equipping of the saints for the work of service, to the building up of the body of Christ." The focus of this chapter is the office of evangelist, but the other offices will be considered in order to understand the office of evangelist. Let it also be noted that there are differing views concerning the office of pastor/teacher and whether it is only one office or two. There are also those who include the deacon in the list of church offices. However, it is not the purpose herein to address these issues but rather to simply observe the offices listed in Ephesians 4:11 only insofar as they shed light on the office of evangelist.

Before continuing, some context is necessary. God's visible covenant people have always been ruled by elders. The governmental framework of Presbyterianism, rule by elders, is not a New Testament idea. That God has used elders in the governance of his people throughout history is clear from the biblical record.[1] It is no surprise, then, that this continues in the New Testament church. God has always governed his people through representative elders who act on behalf of the people in the prescribing of God's ordinances as received from him and the execution of the means of grace, such as the ceremonial law of the Old Testament and the sacraments of the New Testament. Rule by elders was the accepted reality among the early church at the time Paul wrote to the Ephesians.

Therefore, it is my argument that all of the offices listed in Ephesians 4:11 fall into the general eldership category. The four positions mentioned were the four functions of the eldership at that time. In order to shed light on the third one, I will address the first two and then the last one and their roles within the church. First, though, it should be noted that all elders at the time fell into one or more of the four categories. All elders functioned in at least one of those four offices. However, not everyone exercising those gifts necessarily operated as an elder. In other words, all elders were apostles, prophets, evangelists, and/or pastors and teachers; but not everyone who exercised the gifts of apostle, prophet, evangelist,

---

1. Exod 24; Lev 4:15; Num 11; Josh 8:10; Judg 2:7; Ruth 4; 1 Sam 16:4; 2 Kgs 19:2; Jer 26:17; Ezek 20:1; Joel 2:16; Matt 15:2; Acts 4:8.

and/or pastor and teacher was automatically an elder. Meaning, it was possible for someone to prophesy without being a prophet (viz., John 11:51), do evangelism without being an evangelist, or teach without being a teacher. Paul is not referring to certain people who may, at times, exercise certain gifts. Rather, he is referring to the specific offices or functions of the ruling elders who were to govern God's people. This is made clear beginning in Ephesians 4:7, where Paul references the grace that was given to each of the saints according to Christ's gift. The context here is the visible church, the body of Christ, and Paul is talking about grace coming to every member of the body through Christ's gift. In Ephesians 4:11, Paul outlines the gift of Christ through which grace is administered to his people. The gift of Christ is, namely, the various functions of the eldership. Paul then continues in Ephesians 4:12, saying that all this is "for the equipping of the saints for the work of service, to the building up of the body of Christ."

So, Paul has in mind here something that is for all the saints and that serves to build up the whole of the body of Christ. This necessarily excludes certain people who, at times, exercise particular gifts for the benefit of particular people. While a gifted woman teaching her children and other women in the church is a God-given blessing, it is a blessing given for the building up of particular people, as opposed to the building up of the entire body of Christ. Paul has in mind here the ordained office of elder that has served and continues to serve the building up of the whole of God's visible people; and in Ephesians 4:11, he mentions the four functioning operations of the eldership at that time. To this we now turn, keeping in mind that the ultimate purpose of all four was the same—the building up of the body of Christ.

The Offices of Apostle, Prophet, and Pastor/Teacher

The elders who served as apostles for the building up of the body of Christ were those men who were commissioned by Christ to set the foundation of the church (viz., 1 Cor 3:10; Eph 2:20; Rev 21:14) and pass down once and for all the words spoken beforehand by the holy prophets and the commandment of the Lord (viz., 2 Pet 3:2; Jude 1:3). This was done mostly through the writing of the New Testament canon as the apostles remembered the things that Christ spoke to them (viz., John 14:26) and wrote down that which Christ commanded them to write (viz., Rev 1:1–2) and also through verbal preaching and teaching (viz., Acts 2, 19:9–10). This function of the eldership necessarily ceased in the first century, because the apostles were, by definition, commissioned by Christ and given the job of building the foundation of the church. It should be noted, though, that not all churches had elders who were apostles. Proportionally, there were only a few apostles, while there were many churches.

The elders who served as prophets for the building up of the body of Christ were those men who, again, helped lay the foundation of the church (viz., Eph 2:20) through the proclamation, both verbal and written, of that which God had spoken directly to them. Prophecy functioned identically under the old covenant as it did at the time Paul wrote to the Ephesian church. Peter made this clear when he united the Old and New Testaments in Acts 2 by saying that the outpouring of the Holy Spirit at Pentecost was a fulfillment of the prophesy in Joel 2. Prophets were for the edification and exhortation of the church, speaking that which God revealed to them (viz., 1 Cor 14:6). All apostles served as prophets in that they relayed that which Christ had spoken to them, but not all prophets were apostles. As stated above, not all churches had access to the apostles in the first century and were, thus, left wanting of the will of God as it was progressively revealed. This is why, as Ephesians 2:20 states, the household of God was built on the foundation of the apostles and the prophets. The apostles had the word of God as spoken to them by Christ himself, and the prophets had the word of God as spoken to them through direct revelation. The word of God as revealed through the apostles and prophets, then, was the foundation upon which the church was built. Like the function of the apostle, the function of the prophet also ceased once the revelation of God had been perfected or accomplished with the completion of the New Testament canon (viz., 1 Cor 13:8–10). The church is no longer dependent upon the partial prophesy of men, for the complete revelation of the will of God pertaining to all matters of faith and practice has been given to the church in the form of the Bible and can be approached objectively. Saints no longer have to go to the prophet to inquire of God's opinion concerning something. They only have to open and read the pages of Scripture.

The elders who served as pastors and teachers for the building up of the body of Christ were those men appointed within every church (viz., Acts 13:23; Titus 1:5) to shepherd the flock by guarding against false doctrine (viz., 1 Tim 4:6) and holding fast the faithful word (viz., Titus 1:9). This is the one function of the eldership that must be present in every church. These are the men charged to preach the word—namely, in reproof, rebuke, and exhortation with much patience and instruction (viz., 2 Tim 4:2). They apply the word of God to their flock and watch over their spiritual well-being (viz., Heb 13:17). All elders necessarily fall into this category, for being able to teach is listed as a universal prerequisite for an elder (viz., 1 Tim 3:2; 2 Tim 2:24). This is the reason all churches must have the office of pastor/teacher and why the office has remained in the postapostolic age.

The Office of Missionary/Evangelist

We now turn to the third office listed in Ephesians 4:11, the office of missionary/evangelist. I call it the "office of missionary/evangelist" as opposed to just the "office of evangelist" because the missionary office is a subset of the office of evangelist; and our concern is with the office of missionary, which makes it necessary to deal with the office of evangelist in general before we deal with the office of missionary in particular. I call the office of missionary a "subset of the office of evangelist" because all missionaries are necessarily evangelists, but not all evangelists are necessarily missionaries. This distinction will be dealt with shortly, but we shall first deal with the general office of evangelist.

The elders who served as evangelists for the building up of the body of Christ were those men commissioned by Christ (viz., Matt 28:18–20; Acts 1:8) or the church (viz., Acts 13:3) to preach the good news of the gospel of Jesus Christ (viz., Acts 8:4). Like all elders, these were ordained men set apart for the purpose of bestowing grace upon the saints through the building up of the church. They too were required to be able to teach and handle the word of God accurately. Where the function differs is in its focus, which is, namely, on the proclamation of the gospel. All newly organized churches require the presence of an evangelist in order for the gospel to take root (viz., Col 1:6–7), but established churches can survive without an elder functioning as an evangelist. This is why passages such as 1 Corinthians 12:28 mention apostles, prophets, and teachers, while omitting evangelists. However, some established churches must have elders operating as evangelists, because evangelists necessarily come from established churches. The office of evangelist is, therefore, a nonessential office that continues in the postapostolic age. By "nonessential," I do not mean that evangelists are not needed. I only mean that they are not needed for the functioning of an established church.

There are only two accounts in Scripture that actually refer to an individual as an evangelist. The first is in Acts 21:8, where Paul entered "the house of Philip the evangelist, who was one of the seven." The reference to Philip being one of the seven is a reference to Acts 6, where seven men from among the brethren of the disciples were selected to serve tables. This makes the Philip of Acts 21 the same Philip as in Acts 8, who began proclaiming Christ in the city of Samaria (viz., Acts 8:4–5), preached Jesus to the Ethiopian eunuch (viz., Acts 8:35), and continued preaching the gospel in all the cities until he came to Caesarea (viz., Acts 8:40). In fact, all of Acts 8 is a record of Philip's evangelistic ministry. Philip went to Samaria, a place where the church had not yet spread, and preached the good news of the kingdom of God in the name of Jesus Christ (viz., Acts 8:12). The Lord sent him "to the road that descends from Jerusalem to Gaza" in order to preach to the Ethiopian (Acts 8:26). The Spirit of the Lord then snatched Philip away and brought him to Azotus, and he preached the gospel in all the cities until he came to Caesarea (viz., Acts 8:39–40). As one can see, the ministry of Philip the evangelist was focused primarily on the preaching of the gospel. However, it should be noted that some twenty years passed between Philip's arrival in Caesarea in Acts 8 and when Paul entered Philip's house in Caesarea in Acts 21. Presumably, Philip remained in Caesarea that entire time. This indicates that the office of evangelist focuses on the proclamation of the gospel but does not work exclusively among unbelievers.

This reality is also clearly seen in the Bible's second reference to an evangelist. In 2 Timothy 4:5, Paul writes to Timothy, saying, "But you, be sober in all things, endure hardship, do the work of an evangelist, fulfill your ministry." Doing the work of an evangelist is included in the fulfillment of Timothy's ministry. Paul also exhorts him not to be ashamed of the testimony of the Lord but to join with Paul in suffering for the gospel (viz., 2 Tim 1:8) and to entrust to faithful men the things that he had heard from Paul (viz., 2 Tim 2:2). Under the umbrella of the work of an evangelist, then, is a passion for the testimony of Christ to the point of suffering on account of the gospel and a handing down to faithful men the teachings of the apostles. This can take place, first, among unbelievers with the initial preaching of the gospel, as seen in Acts 8, and, second, within an established church such as at Ephesus, as those who have responded to the message of the gospel are taught to obey all that Christ has commanded. Therefore, an elder holding the office of evangelist focuses his preaching on the proclamation of the gospel but is also ready to feed the saints with the whole counsel of God's word.

The Evangelist As a Missionary

With the general function of the office of evangelist defined, we can now turn to the particular subset of the office of missionary. It should be noted that everything that is true and required of an evangelist is also true and required of a missionary. He must meet the qualifications of an elder and be ordained by the church and set apart for the purpose of preaching the gospel for the building up of the body of Christ. The difference between the office of missionary and the general office of evangelist has primarily to do with those among whom the missionary preaches.

While the term "missionary" or "missions" was popularized by the Jesuits in the late 1500s when they sent members abroad, it originates from the Latin word *missio*, which means "to send." Variations of this word are found in the Latin Vulgate, referring to the disciples and/or apostles being sent. In Matthew 10:16, Christ said to the disciples, "Behold, I send (*missio*) you out as sheep in the midst of wolves." Mark 6:7 states that Christ "summoned the twelve and began to send (*missio*) them in pairs, and gave them authority over unclean spirits." Jesus said to the disciples in John 20:21, "As the Father has sent (*missio*) Me, I also send (*missio*) you." So, the core meaning of *missio*, or "missions," is "to send" or "to be sent." However, there is more to the biblical definition of "missions," for the emphasis in the text is not simply that sending is taking place. Rather, the emphasis is on to whom the person is being sent and what it is that he is being sent to do. Paraphrasing Christ's statement regarding him in Acts 9:15, Paul is quoted in Acts 22:21 as saying, "And He said to me, 'Go! For I will send you far away to the Gentiles.'" Paul states explicitly in 1 Corinthians 1:17 that Christ sent him "to preach the gospel." As a missionary, therefore, Paul was sent to the Gentiles in order to preach the gospel. The Greek word translated as "Gentiles" is *ethnos*, and it literally means "nations." While the Latin *missio* is not found in Christ's commissioning of his disciples just prior to his ascension in Matthew 28, Luke 24, or Acts 1, these passages have come to symbolize the missionary calling, as they do contain the commissioning of the disciples to go throughout all the nations preaching the gospel.

With this definition as the foundation, a missionary is an elder who is sent by Christ or his church to preach the gospel among the nations. Later chapters will address the manner in which he is sent, what it means to preach the gospel, and who the nations are, so not much detail will be presented here about role of the missionary. Suffice it to say that the particular function of the missionary is to preach the gospel among the nations. This is where the distinction between the missionary and the evangelist is found. Both are ordained elders with the particular focus of preaching the gospel. The evangelist may preach the gospel among unbelievers, within an established church, or a combination of the two. The missionary may also, throughout the duration of his career, preach the gospel initially among unbelievers and then within an established church as God's elect respond in faith to the initial preaching, but the missionary is sent to do this among the nations. He preaches the gospel among other peoples because Christ has purchased for God, with his blood, men from every tribe and tongue and people and nation. The evangelist is to preach the gospel wherever he finds himself, but the missionary is to continually push his preaching to the ends of the earth so that "they who had no news of Him shall see, And they who have not heard shall understand" (Rom 15:21; Isa 52:15).

We now have a brief yet biblical understanding of the role of the missionary. He is an ordained elder who is to preach the gospel among the nations. As stated at the beginning of the chapter, however, this understanding is often neglected or rejected outright within the modern church. This has led to a gross misunderstanding of the missionary office, leaving ambitious saints stunned by hardships and the nations wanting of the gospel.

The Unnecessary Atrocities Resulting from the Neglect of the Office of Missionary

Having seen with my own eyes men and women swallowed up by the pitfalls associated with the neglect of the doctrine of the office of missionary, I am compelled to take a moment here and denounce the activities and people that try to sneak into the category of missions. To put it most bluntly, if something does not contain the proclamation of the gospel among the nations, it is not missions. If a person is not ordained by the church to preach the gospel among the nations, he is not a missionary. All activities, whether foreign or domestic, that do not have as their primary purpose the spread of the gospel among the nations, do not constitute missions. The building of orphanages, digging of wells, teaching and feeding of children, caring for the infirmed, and all other social services are not, in and of themselves, missions. Anyone who goes or is sent to the nations to participate in these social services is not, on the basis of such service alone, a missionary.

Now, I must be careful, because the reader is liable to hear something that I am not saying. First, nothing has been mentioned here of the benevolence of these activities and those who participate in them. In fact, these actions are of great value, and Christians ought to be involved in them. Second, I have not said that missions cannot or does not contain these things. Missions can contain all the various types of social service, but such services always serve the ultimate goal of preaching the gospel. Luke was a physician who undoubtedly provided care for some people during his journeys throughout Asia Minor and Greece, but that was not the primary reason why he traveled with Paul. My only point is that these activities, while good and beneficial, do not represent missions or make the doer of them a missionary.

The unfortunate reality is that men and women are sent throughout the world to do good things for people, and they are told that this will somehow fulfill the Great Commission and bring about the consummation of the Great Enterprise with the ingathering of all God's elect from among the nations. The unfortunate part is not that good things are being done throughout the world but rather that men and women are duped into believing that they are acting in obedience to Matthew 28:18–20. These misled saints lay hold of Christ's claim that all authority in heaven and on earth is his and that he will be with them always, and they go out to care for a fallen and broken world. The problem is that babies still die. Disease continues to spread. Famine is not wiped out. Needless wars break out. Men continue to abuse and victimize each other in atrocious ways. The problems that these saints go out to fix only get worse, and they are left wondering why the God who claimed to have all authority and to be with them forever actually abandoned them. The nations, at the same time, not only continue to endure the hardships that befall all of humanity, but they do so without any hope of salvation as the gospel is truncated into social services. This is a pitiful atrocity that ought not be.

There is yet another miserable side effect to this situation. There are those in the church who are apt to read God's word for themselves and discern that missions has to do ultimately with the proclamation of the gospel among the nations. Trying to bring clarity to the sea of confusion that surrounds the Great Commission, they boldly step out with ambition to preach the gospel among the nations. Churches, however, toss these ambitious brothers back into the stale sea of modern missions and treat them like all the other philanthropic social workers. This leaves these men without the biblical authority to preach the gospel and organize churches through the exercising of the means of grace and the appointing of elders. One of two undesirable consequences inevitably comes from this. One, the brother finds himself beaten by the enemy in the same way as the seven sons of Sceva in Acts 19:14–16, who had no authority to preach the gospel and were sent away naked and wounded. Two, the brother finds success among certain people; but the converts are left isolated from the body of Christ because no church can exist without the office of elder, which can only be established by other elders. The best these ambitious brothers can hope for is that they make converts who are then essentially orphaned to the world without any access to the church or the means of grace. This too is a pitiful atrocity that ought not be.

Another calamitous byproduct of the widespread misunderstanding of the office of missionary and its function is the notion that each saint is a missionary and that missions can be done in one's neighborhood or workplace. This concept has two negative consequences; and what makes it so dangerous is that, while these consequences are ultimately devastating, they are not immediately realized, making the concept likely to linger. The first consequence is that saints are robbed of the opportunity to participate in the Great Enterprise. They are deceived into believing that inviting their neighbor over for dinner is somehow related to Matthew

28:18–20. They will later come to the end of their lives expecting to hear, "Well done, good and faithful servant." Instead, they will be confronted with the reality that they lived most of their lives for a lie. The second consequence is that while churches and their people invest their time and resources into their own communities, the nations remain separated from any hope of salvation, and the worship that Christ deserves from them is not received.

The Solution

The solution is quite clear and quite simple. The nations are in desperate need of ordained elders to be sent to preach the gospel and organize churches throughout the entire world, and Christian philanthropy needs to be called exactly what it is and not treated as something it is not. With this distinction, missionaries can execute the church's role within the Great Enterprise under and with the authority of the church—the authority that has been bestowed upon the elders. Social workers can embrace the Great Commandment to love thy neighbor as thyself and know that Christ does have all authority and will not abandon his people (viz., 2 Tim 2:13), even though poverty and famine will always plague the earth (viz., Matt 26:11). In this way, "the manifold wisdom of God might now be made known through the church to the rulers and the authorities in the heavenly places" (Eph 3:10).

God's elders must now give consideration to these things. They must consider whether they have neglected to recognize and ordain men who are called to function as missionaries, have truncated missions into social service, or have neglected the possibility that they themselves may be called to function in the office of missionary—all of which continue to leave the nations wanting of the power of God for salvation. Only when God's elders begin to provide the difficult answers to these uneasy questions will the church cease to wound her people and limp along within the Great Enterprise.

four

The Missionary Calling and the Setting Apart of the Missionary

This chapter has to do with the inward and outward call of the missionary. By "inward call," I mean that internal conviction felt by the missionary that he is to dedicate his life to the spread of the gospel among the nations. By "external call," I mean the act in which the local church recognizes such a call in the life of the missionary and sets him apart for the work of service. This chapter first addresses the inward call, namely, what it is and what it is not. Second, this chapter addresses the manner in which this calling is recognized within the church and the manner in which the missionary is set apart.

The Inward Call

While it is accurate to define the inward call as that internal conviction felt by the missionary, this definition is also wholly insufficient, for it does not reveal the foundation in which this conviction must be rooted. As the missionary's life is one with high stakes, his conviction must be rooted in unshakable ground, and anything other than the word of God will not provide such a footing. The missionary must be convinced of his calling through the Scriptures. Otherwise, the ground on which he stands will eventually give way to the erosion brought on by the deception of the enemy, whether the enemy be the missionary's own flesh or the powers that have the authority to wage war with the saints.

The Missionary Calling and the Setting Apart of the Missionary

The written word of God is the surest foundation upon which anything can be built, and it must be the foundation upon which the missionary conviction is fostered. To make this point clear, one must only look to Paul's writing. In Romans 15, he states his ambition for missionary service by saying that he has fully preached the gospel all the way from Jerusalem to Illyricum and, thus, aspires "to preach the gospel, not where Christ was already named" (Rom 15:20). He then goes on to state the reason for his ambition. Remember, this is the man who was met by Christ on the road to Damascus. Concerning Paul, Christ said in Acts 9:15, "He is a chosen instrument of Mine to bear My name before the Gentiles and kings and the sons of Israel." Could there be any greater call than the risen Christ speaking of Paul and to Paul personally? There are many saints today who think the Christian life would be easier if Christ were standing in front of them, telling them what to do. This, however, represents a gross misunderstanding of God's communication with mankind, for Paul did have Christ standing in front of him and telling him what to do. Yet, Paul still grounded himself and his calling in the written word of God.

After stating his ambition for missionary service in Romans 15, Paul goes on to quote Isaiah 52:15 as the basis for his ambition. The context in Romans is that Paul is wrapping up his theological discourse and introducing a personal tone to the letter by expressing his desire to visit Rome in passing while on his way to preach the gospel in Spain; and in Romans 15:24, he states the reason he wants to see them, saying, "For I hope to see you in passing, and to be helped on my way there by you." So, Paul wants to be helped by the church in Rome on his way to preach the gospel in Spain, and he has decided that sharing his missionary ambition and the reason for it is the best way to get the church in Rome to actually help him in his endeavor to reach Spain. At this point, Paul goes to the bedrock of the foundation of his missionary conviction, wanting to show the church in Rome as clearly and substantively as possible the firmness and surety of his calling. Amazingly, though, he does not go to his experience on the road to Damascus. Rather, he quotes from Isaiah. For those with eyes to see, this is stunning. Paul elevates the written word of God above that which Christ personally spoke about him. This is the man who was caught up to the third heaven (viz., 2 Cor 12:2) and raised a boy from the dead (viz., Acts 20:10), yet he quotes an Old Testament prophet in hopes of getting the church in Rome to help him get to Spain.

The Great Enterprise from a Reformed Perspective

After stating his aspirations for reaching Spain, he then says in Romans 15:21, "But as it is written, 'They who had no news of Him shall see, And they who have not heard shall understand.'" This is a quote from the second half of Isaiah 52:15. As shown in chapter 2, what had not been told them and what they had not heard is revealed in Isaiah 52:9–10, which says, "Break forth, shout joyfully together, You waste places of Jerusalem; For the Lord has comforted His people, He has redeemed Jerusalem. The Lord has bared His holy arm In the sight of all the nations, That all the ends of the earth may see The salvation of our God." What the nations have not yet heard is that God has bared his holy arm so that all the ends of the earth may see the salvation of God. In case the servant of God being lifted up in Isaiah 52:13 and the nations being sprinkled with his blood in Isaiah 52:15a is not enough to convince the naysayer that baring his holy arm is a reference to Christ, Isaiah makes it explicitly clear in Isaiah 53. This is a prophetic passage depicting Christ's crucifixion, and Isaiah makes clear that the arm of the Lord is he who "grew up before Him like a tender shoot" (v. 2), "was despised and forsaken of men" (v. 3), "was pierced through for our transgressions" (v. 5), "was oppressed" (v. 7), and was crushed by the Lord and rendered "Himself as a guilt offering" (v. 10). The Lord was indeed pleased to crush him, and he did it in the sight of the nations so that all the ends of the earth would see his salvation (viz., Isa 52:10) and that all nations and tongues would come and see the glory of God (viz., Isa 66:18).

This is the foundation of Paul's missionary conviction in Romans 15:20–21, and it is more certain than Christ's personal words because it encompasses the whole of the Great Enterprise. By quoting Isaiah, Paul puts himself squarely in the middle of what God has been up to since the beginning of time. He does not want the church in Rome to help him because the risen Christ gave him some special assignment. Rather, he wants the church in Rome to help him because he is a cog in the millennia-long wheel that God has set in motion in order to cover the earth with the knowledge of the glory of the Lord (viz., Hab 2:14). The missionary must also, then, find his conviction in the written word of God and place himself squarely in the middle of what God has been up to since the beginning of time.

There is now a pertinent question that must be raised. How is the missionary to find his own calling in the pages of the Bible? In other words, is Isaiah 52:15 only for Paul, or does it apply to others? If it applies to others, does it apply to everyone or just certain people? If it only applies to certain people, how is it to be known to which people it applies? How is the missionary calling to be rooted in Scripture?

As stated previously, the inward call is something internal. No one is able to receive it or go and get it. One either has it or not. The task is in recognizing it when it is present, much like an artist recognizes his love for and ability to create art. One might argue that an artist knows he is an artist because of the art he has produced, but what about the internal creative nature of the artist prior to creating his first work of art? Did the artist then know that he was an artist? Was he then inclined to creative imagination? Indeed, there is something innate in the artist that he recognizes when the proper light is shown thereon. In the same way, there is something innate in the missionary that he recognizes when the proper light is shown thereon. The proper light, in this context, is the Bible. Michelangelo looked at a slab of marble and saw the Renaissance masterpiece *David* and was compelled to sculpt it. The missionary looks at the Scriptures and sees the Great Enterprise and is compelled embark up on it. Only the artist is compelled to carve out a marble masterpiece from beneath the surface, and only the missionary is compelled by God's written word to take the gospel to the ends of the earth.

All saints fit into one of two categories. They are either compelled to go to the ends of the earth, just as Paul was compelled to go to Spain; or they are compelled to help those going to the ends of the earth along the way, just as the Philippian church (viz., Phil 4:14) helped Paul and as, presumably, the church in Rome would have helped him, given the opportunity. If someone is compelled to go, he should test the foundation of his desire and see whether his footing is sure. If his footing is sure, then he should begin looking for opportunities to express his calling.

Testing One's Footing

Looking for such opportunities moves us into the realm of the outward call, but we must first address the testing of the foundation before moving on from the inward call. Isaiah's prophecy that all the ends of the earth would see the salvation of God is what compelled Paul to preach the gospel among the nations. There were surely other influences that spurred him along the way. It requires no stretch to imagine Paul wanting to render some kind of restitution for the abuse he had previously inflicted upon the church; but this and all other superfluous influences were always contained within his biblical conviction, not the other way around. While recognizing the vast array of influences, the missionary must scrutinize them all and learn which one lies at the bottom of his conviction.

Christ's instruction to his disciples in Matthew 9:37–38 and Luke 10:2 to beseech the Lord to send out workers into the harvest is a good place to start. When a saint who is not a missionary reads this, he identifies with the one instructed to pray. When a missionary saint reads this, he identifies both with the one instructed to pray and also with the workers being sent into the harvest. When one envisions in his mind workers going out into the harvest, does he see them going out from where he is, or does he see himself among those sent into the harvest? If he sees himself amongst the workers, this may be evidence of the inward missionary calling.

I say that it may only be evidence of this calling, because it could also be evidence of something else. This depends on what it is that he sees himself and the other workers doing. There are many things that could cause him to see himself as one of the workers. Some saints love to travel and are, therefore, inclined to picture themselves going out. Some love the study of and the interaction with other cultures and are, therefore, inclined to picture themselves going out. Some are compelled to care for orphans and are, therefore, inclined to picture the harvest as orphans awaiting a caretaker. Some are compelled to relieve famine and are, therefore, inclined to see the harvest as the starving populations of the world. Some are moved by the awful injustices of the world, like the sex trafficking that takes place in Southeast Asia, and are, therefore, inclined to see the harvest as victimized women waiting desperately for deliverance. Some are motivated by a compassion for the infirmed of the world and are, therefore, inclined to see the harvest as the sick and suffering waiting for proper care. Traveling the world and addressing these issues would all be legitimate endeavors that saints are free to embark upon. However, none of them constitute missions, and they must not be the bedrock of the missionary calling. Only a compulsion to take part in the ingathering of God's elect from among the nations through the proclamation of the gospel throughout the world should rest as the anchor of the missionary call. While the activities listed above often do spur the missionary

The Missionary Calling and the Setting Apart of the Missionary

on from time to time, his feet must be planted firmly on the unshakable ground of the Bible and God's Great Enterprise.

For anyone seeking to define the foundation of the missionary calling, there is a substantial amount of biblical passages upon which the missionary can stand. One of those passages will be examined here. Psalm 67 is ripe with missionary statements and bookended by two of the clearest missionary affirmations in all of Scripture. Psalm 67:1–2 says, "God be gracious to us and bless us, And cause His face to shine upon us—That Your way may be known on the earth, Your salvation among all nations." Psalm 67:7 says, "God blesses us, That all the ends of the earth may fear Him." In these three verses, the psalmist clearly states that God is gracious to and blesses his people in order that the nations would know God's way and his salvation. One must consider two things regarding this statement. First, does he agree with it? Does he accept the reality that God has been gracious to him for the purpose that those among the heathen nations would come to fear the Lord, or does he operate under the false notion that God has been gracious to him on account of himself? This question is not restricted to the missionary calling. All saints must address this question. Too many in the modern church spend their lives thinking that God saved them because he longed for their fellowship or was in some way enamored with them. This, according to the psalmist, is very far from the truth. God causes his face to shine upon his people so that the nations will fear him. If one does not accept and embrace this, it is likely that God's face will not shine upon him. Therefore, it behooves all saints to meditate on this truth and come to exult over it.

Second, one must consider the manner in which he has been blessed. Psalm 67:7 states that God blesses his people for the sake of the ends of the earth. This is true for all saints, not just those who are missionaries. God blesses all of his people with gifts and abilities as well as the ambition to use such gifts and abilities in order to achieve the purpose for which they were given. The ultimate end or purpose for all of these gifts is the same, namely, that all nations would know the salvation of God, but the subordinate ends of the gifts vary greatly. If a saint has been blessed with the unique ability to design and build homes, he should design and build homes with all of his heart. If a saint has been blessed with the ability to design computer software, perform delicate brain surgery, provide quality customer service, clean hotel rooms, drive garbage trucks, deliver mail, fly planes, cut wood, sell cars, or any other productive activity in society,

The Great Enterprise from a Reformed Perspective

he should undertake such activity with all of his heart so that he can support the work of God among the nations. However, he should not see Psalm 67 as a calling for him to be a missionary. On the other hand, a saint may be blessed with the unique ability to preach and teach and to endure the hardships associated with living among a foreign people. In this case, Psalm 67 may be calling him to be a missionary. The Scriptures are the light that shines onto the bedrock of every individual's calling in life. If the calling is to be a missionary, the Scriptures will uncover it.

Erosion of the Unsure Calling

Before ending this section on the inward call, it would be unwise not to address the erosion brought on by the deception of the enemy that was referenced earlier. Jesus began the parable of the two builders in Matthew 7:24–27 by saying, "Therefore everyone who hears these words of Mine and acts on them, may be compared to a wise man who built his house on the rock" (v. 24). Before we look at the rest of the parable, it is important to see the context in which the parable is placed. In Matthew 7:13–14, Jesus talked about the narrow way and the fact that few will enter through the narrow gate. In Matthew 7:15–20, Jesus addressed true and false teachers, comparing them to good trees that bear good fruit and bad trees that bear bad fruit. In Matthew 7:21–23, Jesus said that not everyone who addresses him as Lord will enter the kingdom of heaven but rather only those who do not practice lawlessness. The context of the parable, therefore, is a contrast between the right way and the wrong way, true teaching and false teaching, and those who sincerely call Jesus Lord and those who call him Lord but are lawless.

The parable of the two builders is a contrast between the one who follows the narrow way and enters the narrow gate, is aware of false prophets and pays no attention to them, and calls Jesus Lord in accordance with the law, and the one who follows the wide path and enters the wide gate, is not aware of false prophets and is swayed by them, and calls Jesus Lord apart from practicing the law. The parable explains what happens to each builder as a result of the erosion of the foundation upon which he has built his home. In verse 24, hearing the words of Christ and acting upon them is described as building a house upon the rock, and building upon the rock is the only way to avoid the erosion that leads to destruction.

The Missionary Calling and the Setting Apart of the Missionary

Therefore, it behooves the saint to mind the path he is on, beware of false teachers, and call Jesus Lord according to the law of God.

While this parable clearly has to do with God's judgment and wrath upon the unbelieving, the principle it teaches is also applicable to the Christian life, as all saints remain plagued by their flesh and, though counted righteous in Christ, are still prone to wander off the narrow way, pay attention to false teachers, and call Jesus Lord not in accordance with the law. In this case, rain and floods and wind will inevitably come, and the foundation will erode. The unfortunate reality is that many saints have embarked upon missionary activity as a result of wandering off the narrow way, and the house always comes crashing down. In the parable, there are only two options of where to build. There is the rock, and there is sand. There is no middle ground. There is no mixture of limestone and clay. There is only the rock that will hold up that which is built on it through the rain and floods and wind, and there is sand that will always crumble into nothing when assaulted by the rain and floods and wind.

The false teaching that says that caring for starving orphans is a fulfillment of the Great Commission is one of the most common sand pits upon which missionaries build. Erosion comes quickly when the gospel is visibly stagnated and when starving children continue to die. One of the most emotionally painful things for the human eye to see is a child suffering and dying, yet those who care for starving orphans are bound to see it. While God promises success in the Great Commission, he promises nothing concerning the temporal well-being of these children. When missionaries are deceived into thinking that caring for starving orphans is part of the Great Commission, they are deceived into thinking that God has promised physical relief for starving orphans. When the rain and floods and wind of death come crashing down, the sand upon which these missionaries stand dissolves under their feet—leaving them naked, broken, and poor.

Paying attention to false prophets or prophecies is probably the next most common sand pit. My intention here is not to address the issue of the gifts of the Spirit and cessationism. Rather, my intention is only to highlight the necessity of building upon the written word of God. Accepting that there are those within orthodox Christianity who believe in the continuation of the gift of prophecy, I encourage such as these to heed 1 John 4:1, which says, "Beloved, do not believe every spirit, but test the spirits to see whether they are from God, because many false prophets have gone out into the world." Also of importance is Deuteronomy 18:21–22, which says, "You may say in your heart, 'How will we know the word which the LORD has not spoken?' When a prophet speaks in the name of the LORD, if the thing does not come about or come true, that is the thing which the LORD has not spoken." Therefore, one is to test prophets by determining whether the thing that they have spoken comes about. Because prophets and prophecies have to be tested, it can be very destructive to base the missionary call upon them. Suppose a saint is told that God has declared that he is to move to a remote land and preach the gospel, resulting in hundreds of people coming to faith. The only way to know whether the Lord has actually spoken this is to actually move to the remote land and preach. If he makes this the foundation upon which he stands, he must by necessity do so prior to knowing whether or not the words were spoken by God. When the rain and floods and wind come, there may well be hundreds who come to faith. However, he may also be killed, resulting in the condemnation of those people and his family being left alone and desperate. This kind of erosion will wipe away any foundation other than the sure, immutable written word of God.

Even when the missionary stands firmly on the written word of God, he and his family may still be killed, so the reader ought not think that such tragedies are evidence of disobedience or a sandy foundation. This issue will be addressed in the final chapter, but here the point must be made clear that the fate of the missionary is not indicative of his lack of calling. Rather, ensuring the biblical calling is what allows the missionary to endure regardless of his fate.

The Outward Call

Once a saint begins to have the internal conviction that he is to dedicate his life to the spread of the gospel among the nations, he should begin to look for opportunities to express this conviction. This does not mean that he should go out among the nations to preach the gospel and see how it goes. Rather, it means he should express his internal conviction to those in the church of which he is a part. The church can then observe his gifts and objectively confirm or deny his inward conviction. Again, we shall look to Paul as the example.

The Missionary Calling and the Setting Apart of the Missionary

Of importance to the discussion of the outward call is what took place in the years immediately following Paul's conversion. He was met by Christ on the road to Damascus in Acts 9:3–6. He was baptized by Ananias in Acts 9:18. He preached Christ in Damascus in Acts 9:19–22. He escaped Damascus in Acts 9:23–25. According to Galatians 1:17–18, three years passed between Paul's departure from Damascus in Acts 9:25 and his arrival in Jerusalem in Acts 9:26. He associated with the disciples and spoke out boldly in the name of the Lord in Acts 9:26–29, but the brethren sent him away to Tarsus in Acts 9:30. This is the last Paul is heard of in Acts until Acts 11:25, when Barnabas went to Tarsus to find Paul and bring him to Antioch. Paul then taught large numbers of people in Antioch for an entire year (viz., Acts 11:26). Then, the church in Antioch sent a gift to the elders in Jerusalem to help alleviate the famine and sent it in the charge of Barnabas and Paul (viz., Acts 11:30).

Paul provides insight on this time period by saying in Galatians 2:1 that fourteen years passed between his visit to Jerusalem in Acts 9:26 and his being sent back to Jerusalem after his first missionary journey in Acts 15:2, which was three years after his visit to Jerusalem in Acts 11:30. This means there were at least fourteen years between Paul's conversion, when Christ declared that Paul was to be a chosen instrument to bear Christ's name before the Gentiles in Acts 9, and Paul's going to Jerusalem with a gift from the church in Antioch at the end of Acts 11. Over a decade passed, most of which Paul spent in his hometown of Tarsus. Not only had Christ told him that he was to preach to the Gentiles, but he was also a pharisaical student of God's word and undoubtedly knew what Isaiah 52:15 meant for him, yet he simply went home to Tarsus following his conversion and being commissioned by Christ.

Somehow, Barnabas knew that Paul had remained in Tarsus. Given that Barnabas went to look for Paul in the first place and that he then taught considerable numbers as soon as he arrived in Antioch, one must assume that Paul was involved in some kind of preaching and teaching during his time in Tarsus. It is of great significance, though, that Paul was sent to Tarsus (viz., Acts 9:30), remaining there until the one sent to Antioch (viz., Acts 11:22) came and retrieved him. He then stayed in Antioch until he was sent to Jerusalem (viz., Acts 11:30), only returning to Antioch once he had fulfilled his mission in Jerusalem (viz., Acts 12:25). Paul then remained in Antioch, ministering to the Lord along with other prophets and teachers who were there (viz., Acts 13:1-2) until the church prayed for Paul and Barnabas, laid their hands on them, and sent them away (viz., Acts 13:3). Paul had the risen Christ proclaim that he was to be a missionary and was indisputably convinced by Scripture that he was to dedicate his life to the spread of the gospel among the nations, yet he only went where and when he was sent.

Paul's approach to missionary activity reveals a deep respect for the role of the church in recognizing the missionary call in a person's life and setting that individual aside for the work of service. Paul had a most certain internal conviction that he was given grace in order to bring about the obedience of faith among the Gentiles for the sake of Christ's name (viz., Rom 1:5), yet he only embarked upon his missionary work when the church recognized his calling and sent him out. Just as surely as the missionary must have an inward calling based completely on the written word of God, he must also have an outward calling expressed by the church through setting him apart and sending him out. According to Paul's missiology, both the inward and the outward calling are essential.

In response to the church's neglect of the office of missionary, many well-intended saints have embarked upon missionary activity prematurely. The thinking is that if the church does not get on board, then the individual must take things into his own hands. However, Paul waited at least fourteen years for the church to get on board, and he waited patiently. In the same way, well-intended saints with an absolute inward call based solely on the Scriptures must wait patiently for Christ's church to recognize them and send them out. The rest of this chapter looks at the manner in which the church is to recognize such men and set them apart.

Recognizing the Missionary

Paul was sent to Tarsus, brought to Antioch, and sent to Jerusalem, but the first time he was sent to the nations for the purpose of preaching the gospel was in Acts 13:3. As noted earlier, Paul had spent a year with the church in Antioch teaching considerable numbers of people (viz., Acts 11:26). Paul was also deemed worthy, along with Barnabas, of being in charge of the church's gift to the saints in Jerusalem (viz., Acts 11:30). This intimates that Paul demonstrated the ability to teach as well as trustworthiness and the ability to travel long distances among other peoples, all of which are required of the missionary. It can safely be assumed, then, that the church recognized these gifts in Paul, which is why they had no hesitation in sending him when the issue first arose in Acts 13:2.

Paul's story reveals some important principles for the modern church. First, the teachers and prophets in the church in Antioch were the ones who recognized Paul's calling and sent him out. As was seen in chapter 3, the roles of teacher and prophet were functions of the eldership at that time, meaning, that the elders of the church recognized Paul's calling and commissioned him as a missionary. The same is true today. The elders of the church remain the ones with the authority and responsibility to recognize and send out missionaries. Elders are the only ones with the authority to recognize whether someone ought to be set aside and function in the office of missionary. At the same time, elders are also the ones with the responsibility of finding such men and ordaining them with the proper authority to preach the gospel among the nations.

This is not an easy task, and complacency will not serve its realization. The elders of the church in Antioch had no hesitation at all in sending Paul and Barnabas when the issue arose. This means the church had been observing both of them during the year or so that Paul and Barnabas were in Antioch. Elders do not have the luxury of sitting around and waiting for missionaries to appear. Elders must actively look for missionaries within their congregations. Elders must examine all members of their flock for the gifts and abilities necessary for the office of missionary. Elders should know their flock and be aware of the tendencies and callings of every sheep. Unfortunately, too many churches either have too many sheep or not enough elders for this to take place. The result is that God's calling on the lives of his people too often goes unheeded.

When elders do know their flock, there are two ways in which they are to look for the missionary calling in a person. The first way is the way in which Paul was recognized. As soon as he arrived at the church in Antioch, it was clear that he had the gift of teaching. Barnabas already knew it; and the church provided him with plenty of opportunities to demonstrate his gift, resulting in the church having utmost confidence in Paul's ability. Similarly, men who are trained, qualified, and ready may today come into a church after a season of remaining in their own version of Tarsus. In this case, the elders must observe their gift in order to gain confidence and be willing to send them out with the proper authority as soon as the time is right.

The second way in which elders are to look for the missionary calling is with younger men or those new to the faith. Recognizing that these men are not yet ready, elders must still notice in the younger men certain tendencies that indicate the missionary calling and then cultivate these tendencies until the younger men mature to the point that they are qualified for the office of missionary. Again, this is not an easy task, and it requires considerable diligence. An example of this is Paul's cultivation of Timothy. Paul first found Timothy during his second missionary journey in Derbe and Lystra in Acts 16:1. As Timothy was well spoken of by the brethren (viz., Acts 16:2), Paul wanted to take Timothy with him. Timothy is mentioned five more times in Acts, each mention referring to his accompanying Paul. Nowhere in Acts is Timothy spoken of as actually preaching or exercising any kind of authority; yet in many of the letters Paul wrote during that time, Timothy was included as one of the authors. This suggests that while Timothy had not yet matured enough to hold the office of evangelist, Paul took him under his wing and cultivated in him the gifts necessary for the office of evangelist.

Timothy apparently stayed with Paul throughout the remainder of Acts and was with Paul during his first imprisonment in Rome. This, along with Timothy's maturation, is seen in Philippians 2:19–22, where Paul says to the Philippian church, "But I hope in the Lord Jesus to send Timothy to you shortly . . . For I have no one else of kindred spirit who will genuinely be concerned for your welfare . . . But you know of his proven worth, that he served with me in the furtherance of the gospel like a child serving his father." Seen here is that Timothy proved his worth by serving Paul like a father. This implies that Paul treated Timothy as a son. Many fathers know what it is like to raise a son, and this is exactly the way in which elders are to develop and nurture the missionary calling within younger men. Paul took note of Timothy when he was just a young lad in Lystra and then dedicated himself to Timothy the way a father is dedicated to a son, resulting in Timothy's maturation and ordination as an elder (viz., 1 Tim 4:14).

The Ordination of the Missionary

This leads to the final point of this chapter. With the inward call solidified and recognized by the elders, the missionary must then be ordained and set apart for the work of service. As shown in chapter 3, the missionary must have the authority to preach the gospel and organize a church. This authority is bestowed upon God's elders, meaning, that the missionary must be ordained as an elder. It is the responsibility of God's elders not only to recognize men with a missionary calling but also to appropriately ordain them with the proper authority so that they can properly execute their ministry. Without this final step, the missionary call goes unfulfilled.

This is quite different from the modern idea of sending out missionaries. Somehow, the notion has arisen that missionaries recognize themselves and go with the blessing of a church, but they are not sent with that church's authority. The brightest minds and most effective preachers are kept at home, while those not seen as fit for the pastorate are sent to the nations. This could be due to churches' selfishness in wanting to keep the best shepherds for themselves but certainly points to elders' unwillingness to recognize missionaries as officeholders within the church. In order to rectify this problem, those men with missionary ambition who are biblically qualified must be ordained as elders and sent to preach the gospel among the nations, and churches must be willing to send their brightest and best to the ends of the earth.

five

Supporting the Missionary

ONE OF THE UNFORTUNATE realities for modern missionaries is the plague of being forced to fundraise. Not only is lack of funding the greatest obstacle to getting missionaries into the field, it also continues to handicap them once they are in the field. Missionaries, by definition, are gifted evangelists and preachers, not fundraisers, and it is a tragedy that so many of them are forced to spend so much of their time and energy securing the financial resources needed to take the gospel to the ends of the earth. This leaves little time for preaching Christ where he has not yet been preached. However, when missionaries spend less time fundraising, they have less money to live on and can often be troubled by the anxieties of the world.

There are very few churches and mission agencies that actually support the missionaries they send. The Southern Baptists' International Mission Board is one agency that does actually take care of its missionaries. Sadly, though, this is the exception and not the rule. The fault, however, lies not with mission agencies but instead with sending churches. Mission agencies are not sending entities and are, therefore, not responsible for supporting missionaries. Churches, in contrast, are sending entities and are, therefore, responsible for supporting the missionaries they send. Mission agencies fulfill a vital role by acting as facilitators. They offer an incredible pool of resources (cultural, linguistic, and strategic) that aid missionaries in their endeavors. So, nothing written in this chapter is aimed at criticizing mission agencies. Rather, the aim of this chapter is to uncover for the church the biblical model of supporting missionaries.

The point of chapter 3 was to show that missionaries are to be officeholders in the church and that they are elders by definition. As was also addressed in chapter 3, the rejection of this doctrine has had numerous consequences, one of which is that churches have come to the conclusion that they are not responsible for the financial well-being of their missionaries. There are various ways to categorize elders. Chapter 3 categorized them according to their function. Here, they will be categorized according to their being subject to the dominion mandate and its requirement to produce goods and capital or to their having the Lord as their inheritance in the same way the Levites did under the old covenant (viz., Num 18:20). In other words, there are elders who are to support themselves financially, and there are elders who are to be supported financially by the church. This chapter will clearly show which category the missionary falls into and address churches' responsibility to support the missionaries they send out.

The Dominion Mandate

The aim here is not to address the doctrine of the dominion mandate and whether or not it includes procreation, whether Christ fulfilled it, or if the church is charged with fulfilling it. Nor is the aim to discuss whether or not elders under the new covenant have taken the place of the Levites under the old covenant. While such topics make for worthwhile discussion, they are not pertinent to the purpose herein. Rather, the purpose here is to examine which elders are responsible for their own financial well-being and which ones have their inheritance in the church in the same way that the Levites had the Lord as their portion. In this way, we will be able to determine who is responsible for the financial support of missionaries.

By saying that someone is subject to the dominion mandate, I simply mean that he is to work for a living either by creating capital himself or providing services for someone else who creates capital. Initially, all of humanity was subject to this mandate. This is found in Genesis 1:28, which says, "God blessed them; and God said to them, 'Be fruitful and multiply, and fill the earth, and subdue it; and rule over the fish of the sea and over the birds of the sky and over every living thing that moves on the earth.'" Successive to the fall in the garden of Eden, God added to the mandate, saying in Genesis 3:17–19, "Cursed is the ground because of you; In toil you will eat of it All the days or your life. Both thorns and thistles it shall grow for you; And you will eat the plants of the field; By the sweat of your face You will eat bread." So, God gave dominion over the earth to man and then ordained that man work and toil in order to garner produce for the sustenance of himself and his family. Paul taught this in the early church (viz., 2 Thess 3:10–12), and the idea has continued throughout history. However, there was an exception found within the tribe of Levi. When the land of Canaan was divided among the tribes of Israel, none of the land was designated for the tribe of Levi. This meant they had no land of their own on which to work and toil in order to garner produce and create capital. Furthermore, they were set apart and dedicated to the service of the Lord (viz., Exod 32:29).

The Levitical Exception and Its Continuation in the Church

As the Levites were dedicated to temple service and were without an inheritance in the land, there had to be some other means of supporting them. The practice of tithing (the recognition that a tenth of all first fruits belongs to God; viz., Lev 27:30) had been in place since at least the time of Abraham (viz., Gen 14:18–20). With the establishment of the Levitical priesthood, however, the tithe was included in the Mosaic law as the means of supporting the tribe of Levi. This is clearly seen in Numbers 18:21, which says, "To the sons of Levi, behold, I have given all the tithe in Israel for an inheritance, in return for their service which they perform, the service of the tent of meeting." In this verse, God instituted an exception to the dominion mandate. The Levites were not required to make a living through creating capital or providing services for someone else who created capital. Instead, the Levites were to dedicate themselves to temple service and live off of the tithe of those who made a living through exercising dominion.

This exception continued throughout Israel's history and apparently into the time of the early church. Paul says in 1 Corinthians 9:14, "So also the Lord directed those who proclaim the gospel to get their living from the gospel." The Lord has determined that ministers of the gospel are not to work and toil for a living but instead are to receive their living from the gospel. Paul also writes to Timothy, saying that "elders who rule well are to be considered worthy of double honor, especially those who work hard at preaching and teaching . . . [for] the laborer is worthy of his wages" (1 Tim 5:17–18). These words clearly intimate that elders dedicated to preaching teaching are to be compensated financially for their labor. Elders who work hard at preaching and teaching are unable to work hard at creating capital or providing services, for they are dedicated to the word of God in the same manner as the apostles in Acts 6:2. Clearly, there was an understanding within the early church that some elders were to receive their living by means other than exercising dominion over the earth. Following the tradition of the Levites, elders in the early church also lived off of that which belonged to the Lord—the tithe.

Distinction of Elders

It is important to note, though, that there seems to be a distinction between elders in 1 Timothy 5:17. Two groups of elders are referenced, one of which is distinguished as those who work hard at preaching and teaching. This intimates that there are some elders who do not work hard at preaching and teaching, and the text says that it is the first group that is worthy of wages for work in the church. This is where the Reformed distinction of teaching elders and ruling elders comes from. Evangelical churches have a similar distinction between vocational elders and lay elders. The two traditions use different words, but they mean exactly the same thing. A teaching or vocational elder is one who works hard at or dedicates all of his time to preaching and teaching. Thus, he is to receive his inheritance from the church and is not required to exercise dominion in the creation of capital. A ruling or lay elder is one who does preach and teach but does not dedicate all of his time to the word of God. Reformed circles call this elder a "ruling elder" because, while he does preach and teach, his primary function is in judging matters of doctrine and discipline—hence the term "ruling elder." Evangelical circles call this elder a "lay elder" because, while he is apt to teach, he still works in society under the dominion mandate and does not commit all of his time to the word of God. Regardless of the terms that are used, the distinction is the same. Elders who completely dedicate their time to the word of God are to make their living in the church. Elders who divide their time between the word of God and dominion activities are to toil in the creation of capital along with the rest of humanity.

Here is where the central question of this chapter arises. Into which category does the missionary fall? If all missionaries are elders and if all elders can be categorized into those who labor and toil in the creation of capital for their living or those who work hard at preaching and teaching in the church for their living, in which category of elder does the missionary belong? The answer to this question unequivocally reveals who it is that is responsible for the support of the missionary. Though I have already shown my hand as to what answer I will give, placing the missionary in either category denounces the modern concept of missionary support. According to what has been argued so far, missionaries are either to toil in the creation of capital for their living or are to work hard at preaching and teaching in the church for their living. This necessarily excludes the manner in which the vast majority of modern missionaries earn their living, which is generally through asking people for money. Again, I do not blame missionaries for this. As stated earlier, the blame lies squarely on the shoulders of churches. If missionaries were supported properly, they would not have to go around begging for money. So, regardless of what follows in this chapter, let it be clearly stated that the manner in which modern missionaries raise their support ought not be.

The Missionary As a Teaching or Vocational Elder

As noted in chapter 3, the very definition of the missionary office requires that the missionary be set aside for the work of service. This is seen in Acts 13:2, where the Holy Spirit instructed the church in Antioch to set apart Paul and Barnabas for the work to which they were called. Being set apart and sent away to preach the gospel to the ends of the earth intimates the inability of the missionary to dedicate himself to dominion activity. By definition, he is to work hard at preaching and teaching. Preaching and teaching among the nations is what the missionary does. There is nothing about the role of the missionary that indicates he is to neglect the word of God in order to exercise dominion and create capital. By virtue of his function alone, it is clear that the missionary is to make his living from the gospel and is worthy of his wages in the church.

Supporting the Missionary

Paul makes this explicitly clear in 1 Corinthians 9. He begins the chapter by speaking of his rights as an apostle and elder, saying in verse 6 that he has the right to refrain from working. In verse 7, he uses the analogy of a soldier, asking, "Who at any time serves as a soldier at his own expense?" Thus, Paul clearly implies that it is not the responsibility of the soldier to provide for himself. He continues by quoting the law, saying, "You shall not muzzle the ox while he is threshing" (1 Cor 9:9); and he then exposits the meaning of this statement in verses 10 to 12, saying, "Yes, for our sake it was written, because the plowman ought to plow in hope . . . If we sowed spiritual things in you, is it too much if we reap material things from you? If others share the right over you, do we not more?" Paul is making the case that he has the right to be provided for by the church. As an elder sent to the Gentiles to preach the gospel (viz., 1 Cor 1:17), he had the right to not work and to make his living from the church.

Before continuing, I must make a concession to those who disagree with me. First, I recognize that Paul says in 1 Corinthians 9:15 that he never exercised his right to wages from the church in Corinth. If he did not exercise his right to wages, he must have made a living in some other way. My detractors may use this in arguing that missionaries, like Paul, are not to be a burden to the church and should, thus, support themselves. I also concede that Paul was sent to Corinth, not from the church in Corinth. With my position being that the sending church is responsible for the financial well-being of the missionary, my detractors may argue here that Paul's statements to this non-sending church in 1 Corinthians 9 do not support my argument. As for these two objections, the former will be dealt with later. Concerning the latter, I concede that 1 Corinthians 9 does not support the argument that the sending church is responsible for the financial well-being of the missionary. However, that is not the purpose for which I use 1 Corinthians 9. Rather, I use it to make the case that Paul, as a missionary, claimed he had the right to not work and to be supported by the toil of other saints. In this fashion, 1 Corinthians 9 not only supports my argument but makes the case in an undeniable manner.

At this point, it may be helpful to highlight the complex nature of the relationship between a successful missionary and the various churches with which he has contact. Unlike the pastor, who commits himself to a single flock, the missionary moves from one place to the next as he organizes churches and appoints elders within them. As this process continues, the missionary inevitably develops cherished relationships with numerous churches, many of which may want to participate in sending him to the next place. This is a scenario that is unique to the office of missionary, which is why Paul claimed to have rights to financial wages from various churches. By the time Paul wrote his first letter to the Corinthians, he was in the midst of his third missionary journey; and the church in Corinth was well established, having been organized by Paul during his second missionary journey. So, Paul's comments in 1 Corinthians 9 are in the context of the complex relationship that exists between successful missionaries and the churches within which they have had influence. Prior to the development of these complexities, however, there is only one sending entity, and that entity is the church that ordains and sets the missionary apart for the work to which he is called. When a church ordains someone for the office of missionary, it recognizes that his calling is to work hard at preaching and teaching among the nations. In this recognition, the church agrees that its ordained missionary has a right to be provided for by the church. In this agreement, the ordaining and sending church is responsible for the financial well-being of the missionary. A church does not recognize a man's calling and ordain him to the office of missionary just so that some other entity can provide for him. The initial sending and ordaining church is manifestly and perpetually responsible for the financial well-being of the missionary and his family.

This Responsibility Too Often Avoided

Even among churches that reject the office of missionary, there is a desire, or rather a wish, that they could support their missionaries. The common excuse is that there are just not enough resources to go around. This is true. There are not enough resources to cover all the superfluous expenses that most churches incur. The solution, however, is not to neglect the missionary but rather to align resources with biblical responsibilities. To continue Paul's soldier analogy, how would a general be thought of who recruited a soldier and sent him into battle without any provisions? Churches are guilty of the same thing everyday. They recruit men for service and send them to the ends of the earth without any provisions. This is a great shame, and those charged with keeping watch over the church will give an account for such behavior (viz., Heb 13:17).

Pretending that this problem does not exist will not serve the cause of the Great Enterprise and will leave many well-intended missionaries suffering needlessly on the field. Churches must recognize their role in the ingathering of God's elect from among the nations. Not all saints are to be missionaries. However, all saints are to be a part of a local congregation, and local congregations are to send missionaries to the ends of the earth. Churches have a role to play in the Great Enterprise; and that role is in recognizing, ordaining, sending, and supporting missionaries. This is not the only function of the church, but it is one of the three areas of financial responsibility within the church. If resources are aligned with these three responsibilities, it will ultimately result in the nations singing for joy at the proclamation of the glory of the grace of God.

Where Church Resources Come From

Before outlining the areas of financial responsibility within the church, it is important to make note of where church resources come from. The example of the tithe has already been used in this chapter, but there is great disagreement throughout all the various denominations and traditions within orthodox Christianity as to whether those in the church are required to tithe under the new covenant. Due to the fact that tithing was practiced prior to the Sinaitic covenant, some argue that it is a moral and, thus, perpetual law that is to be observed by all people at all times. Others argue that the law of the tithe was instituted as a ceremonial law under the Sinaitic covenant and was, thus, fulfilled and abrogated by Christ. My purpose here is not to take a position on the doctrine of the tithe but rather to show that giving of some kind is expected within the church.

For those who accept the doctrine of the tithe, it is quite clear where church resources come from. Families subject to the dominion mandate are to give a tenth of their increase to the Lord. Since the Lord is not located somewhere on earth to receive the tenth, it is to be given to his representative elders in the church. Elders are then to allocate such resources according to the biblical prescription.

For those who reject the tithe as a moral law, there is a substantial amount of gray area as to what is expected of saints in the church regarding giving. Some claim that saints are free to give whatever amount they desire to whomever they desire. Others claim that 10 percent is a good

The Great Enterprise from a Reformed Perspective

principle to start with, but it should increase from there. All, however, must agree that some capital gained by saints is to be given to the church so that the church is able to meet its financial responsibilities.

Those lost in a sea of ambiguity regarding this issue should take note of 2 Corinthians 9:8. Tithers will argue that this chapter of Paul's letter is referring only to offerings and is, therefore, not the rule. However, tithers are not lost in a sea of ambiguity. So, this paragraph does not concern them. Everyone else ought to pay attention to what follows. In the context of the chapter, Paul is reminding the Corinthian church of their previously promised gift (viz., 2 Cor 9:5) and is encouraging them to be prepared to make good on their promise. He then makes an unbelievable statement in 2 Corinthians 9:8, saying, "And God is able to make all grace abound to you, so that always having all sufficiency in everything, you may have an abundance for every good deed." Paul says that God is able to make grace abound to the saints, resulting in two things. First, grace abounds so that saints will have sufficiency in everything. Meaning, God will supply them with what is sufficient in everything. God will give them everything they need. Second, grace abounds so that saints will have an abundance for every good deed. Meaning, God will give more than what is merely sufficient; and whatever he gives above what is necessary is to be used for every good work, thus intimating that whatever increase the saints experience above what is sufficient is to be used for the ministry of the church (viz., 2 Cor 9:12).

Regardless of how they view the tithe, everyone must agree that saints are to give financially to the work of the church. The argument is over the amount they are to give. In most cases, God gives more than 10 percent above what is sufficient. So, giving a tenth of the increase is generally the minimum saints should be expected to give, and this minimal amount is sufficient for the church to meet its financial obligations.

Three Areas of Financial Responsibility

As mentioned earlier, one area of financial responsibility is in providing for teaching or vocational elders. This is widely accepted among all the various traditions within orthodox Christianity and, therefore, requires no further discussion. The other two areas, however, are less accepted and

Supporting the Missionary

must be addressed in order to help churches align their resources with biblical responsibilities.

The diaconate is something that is commonly rejected; and if it is not rejected, it is often misunderstood. Though I hold the position that those appointed to serve tables in Acts 6 were of the seventy apostles and were, thus, elders in the church and not deacons, this passage is generally seen as the establishment of the diaconate. Regardless of when it was established, the practice of caring for those in need within the church is referenced frequently in Scripture. According to Acts 6, the church provided food for widows. Paul references a list in 1 Timothy 5:9 in which widows are to be included, and he states in 1 Timothy 5:16 that anyone with a dependent widow must assist her so that the church is not burdened but is able to assist those who are widows indeed. At the very least, this intimates that the church is responsible for assisting some widows. James says in James 1:27 that true and undefiled religion consists of visiting widows and orphans in their distress or tribulation. This seems to be a continuation of what was practiced in Israel under the old covenant. According to the Mosaic law, the tithe of every third year was to be for the Levites, the alien, the orphan, and the widow (viz., Deut 26:12–13). These were those who had no portion in the land and were, therefore, unable to exercise dominion in order to provide for themselves. Under the new covenant, the church has continued to provide for those unable to provide for themselves.

Furthermore, James and John teach that the church is responsible to care for those in need of physical provision. Referring to the evidence of faith, James says that it is of no use to simply speak blessings to someone in need of food and clothing (viz., Jas 2:15). Referring to the expression of God's love, John says that such love does not abide in the heart of him who sees his brother in need and closes his heart against him (viz., 1 John 3:17). This does not apply to the one in need who refuses to exercise dominion and provide for his family (viz., 1 Tim 5:8) but rather only to those who experience extenuating circumstances and find themselves unable to provide for a time. The author of Hebrews praises the church for showing sympathy to those in prison (viz., Heb 10:34). Being imprisoned for Christ is an extenuating circumstance that would render the saint unable to provide for his family for a time. In such case, the church is praised for showing due compassion.

The rejection of the diaconate is a sad reality that exists in many churches. The truth is that certain saints within the church do, at times, have certain rights to financial provision from the church. Some churches do, at times, agree to help those in need, but how many churches have an active list of widows who have rights to financial provision?

Those churches that do not reject the diaconate often misunderstand its purpose. This is particularly true within evangelical circles. There is often an eagerness to help those in need, but such help is directed towards the reprobate at the expense of brothers and sisters in the church. The belief is that caring for the poor and needy will somehow prepare them to receive the gospel, and these churches use the passages listed above as the basis of behaving that way. There is nothing wrong with caring for the poor and needy among the reprobate. The problem arises when the reprobate take precedence over the saints. A church is not responsible for the financial well-being of anyone outside of the congregation. It may, at times, express the love of God towards the poor and needy of the world, but its biblical responsibility is for its own sheep.

The remaining area of financial responsibility within the church is the support of missionaries. As the missionary is a teaching or vocational elder who is to work hard at preaching and teaching, he has no portion in the dominion mandate and must receive his living from the church. This reality is often overlooked because the office of missionary is not an essential office within the church. Every church must have at least one elder. Usually, this one elder is a teaching elder and, thus, receives his living from the church. Every church will also, at times, have saints who are in need. Therefore, churches must maintain the diaconate. However, not every church has an elder who functions as a missionary or an evangelist, so this area of responsibility is easily overlooked. Regardless, many churches do act as sending entities for missionaries and must send them appropriately and provide for their financial well-being.

Realignment of Resources

Any church that sends a missionary but neglects to supply him with the financial resources necessary to execute his calling is continuing in active disobedience to the will of God. I realize this is a tough statement, but churches cannot go on ignoring this reality. The solution, however, is not to cease sending missionaries but rather to realign resources with biblical responsibilities. When the three areas of financial responsibility are taken care of, churches are free to care for the poor and needy among the reprobate, build massive buildings, throw parties, enjoy professional-grade sound systems, or do anything else they choose to do with the capital brought in by the saints. Until that time, however, these things represent an outright rejection of God's direction for provision among those who do not participate in the dominion mandate.

Realigning resources with biblical responsibilities is not very complicated, and it can be done without putting undue burden on the saints. First, financial provision must be provided for the teaching elder or elders. A church with ten tithing families can afford to pay a teaching elder. When this small church includes offerings in addition to tithes (viz., 2 Cor 8:1–6), the diaconate of the church is covered as well. A larger church of twenty or twenty-five families is able, through tithes and offerings, to provide a living for a teaching elder, fund the diaconate, and fully support a missionary. By western standards, this is still a small church; yet in accordance with God's biblical prescription, it can fully support itself and send the gospel to the elect of God who remain scattered across the face of the globe.

Some may argue, though, that I am not being realistic. Churches are forced to incur more expenses than what have been listed here. Many churches have fifty, one hundred, or maybe even one thousand families. Churches of this size need to meet in some kind of facility. They need vans to drive groups to retreats. They need basketball hoops and other games for youth. They need coffee shops in which people can gather. They need curricula for Sunday school. The list goes on and on; and while many church expenses are unfortunate, they are necessary—according to some.

But are they? Are these expenses really necessary? In what building did the church meet in Acts 1? Returning to Jerusalem, the people went up to the upper room where they were staying and with one mind continually devoted themselves to prayer. Then, Peter stood up and addressed the congregation, about 120 persons in total (viz., Acts 1:12–15). This was a church of 120 people, and they met in an upper room. The same was also true of churches in the Gentile lands. In Colossians 4:15, Paul gives instructions to greet the church in the house of Nympha. The whole church was meeting in someone's house. My point is not that the house-church model is the biblical model. My point is simply that buildings are not necessary.

Suppose a church of sixty-five families has facility costs of $4,500 per month. The main purpose of the facility is Sunday worship, which lasts two hours. Some random events take place during the week, but nothing requiring a room that seats three hundred people. Two hours a week comes to eight hours a month. Divide $4,500 by eight hours, and the hourly cost for the facility comes to $562.50. Could a meeting hall not be rented on Sunday mornings for something less than $1,125? Again, I am not saying that churches should not own buildings. I am simply saying that churches should not neglect to provide for their missionaries, and I am pointing out that there are potential solutions.

Due to the fact that few elders and even fewer saints in the church actually see what the missionary endures in the field, most saints are not bothered by the fact that thousands of dollars are spent on lights, projectors, electronics, decorations, paint, new carpet, and heat, while missionaries and their families wonder where their next meal will come from. It is a shame that so many churches are oblivious to the hardships they force the missionary to endure, while saints at home surround themselves with comfort and ease. In the long run, the rewards are so much greater for those who abandon the pursuit of luxury in order to take part in and support the proclamation of the glory of the grace of God throughout the earth. When history is said and done, the quality of the projector in the sanctuary will be inconsequential, but the work of the missionary will be paramount. God's elders must evaluate the appropriation of God's resources and align them with God's directions as laid out in Scripture.

Exceptions to the Rule of Missionary Support

Previously, the objection was raised that Paul did not exercise his right to financial provisions from the church (viz., 1 Cor 9:15) and that modern missionaries should do the same so as to not be a burden to the church, and I conceded that Paul claimed to have the right to financial provisions but chose not to use that right in the case of the Corinthian church. However, this does not mean that other missionaries are to behave in the same way, for Paul did this voluntarily. Paul argues vehemently for his right to financial provisions; but in order to show the sincerity of his preaching, he did not exact from the Corinthian church what was owed him (viz., 1 Cor 9:18). Far from teaching that the missionary is to support himself, this passage actually uncovers an exception to the rule, thus allowing the missionary to voluntarily forgo what the church is responsible for paying. This is not to be asked of the missionary but can only be offered by him.

Various circumstances could perpetuate this forgoing. In the case of the established and successful missionary, there may be a handful of churches desiring to send him forth. Not needing financial support from all of them, he may waive his right to financial provisions from some of them. Though not required to exercise dominion in the creation of capital, the missionary may, at times, perform services or toil in the creation of capital (viz., Acts 18:3). He may have a hobby, such as carpentry or writing, that provides him with financial compensation. In this case, he may willingly forgo some support from the church in order to free up resources for the church's other endeavors. There are also some instances in which a church is actually unable to support the missionary. A church with fifteen families and a teaching elder does not have the resources necessary to support a missionary. This should not exclude such a church from participation in the Great Enterprise; and any missionary called from that church will likely concur with Paul and forgo some financial provision, saying, "I am under compulsion; for woe is me if I do not preach the gospel" (1 Cor 9:16).

Thankfully, God has made biblical exceptions for this scenario. When the church in Antioch sent Paul and Barnabas, it is doubtful that the small church had the resources to fund its diaconate, provide for its teaching elders, and support Paul and Barnabas. This is why Paul accepted and sought gifts from other churches. Writing from prison in Rome, Paul thanks the Philippian church for sending him a gift through Epaphroditus (viz., Phil 4:18). This was not the first time the Philippian church shared with him in the giving and receiving in the cause of the gospel. They sent him gifts more than once during his missionary journeys (viz., Phil 4:15–16). As noted in chapter 4, one of the reasons Paul wrote to the church in Rome was to convince them to support his endeavor to preach the gospel in Spain (viz., Rom 15:24). Churches that did not send Paul were not required to support him, but he did give them the opportunity to partner with him in the Great Enterprise. The same is true today. Churches that do not ordain and send out missionaries are not required to financially support them; but these churches ought to be given the opportunity to participate in the Great Enterprise, should they desire to do so. This exception makes it possible for those churches without an elder functioning in the office of missionary to participate in the Great Enterprise, and for smaller churches with limited resources to send their called and qualified missionaries to the ends of the earth.

Final Words

Some words in this chapter have been admittedly harsh. This is not my intention. I long for the day when I can write about the incredible success churches are finding as they participate in the Great Enterprise. I really do love the church and all of her visible manifestations. This is why I have written these things. I want the church to realize her place in the Great Enterprise and boldly embrace it. We will have eternity to be comfortable and live in luxury, but that time has not yet come. We have brothers and sisters spread across the globe, throughout all the various peoples of the earth, who are desperately waiting for the gospel, and there are qualified men eager to preach to them. Nothing should hinder these men from going, especially not a lack of finances. God owns the cattle on a thousand hills, yet churches do not send missionaries due to a lack of resources. There is something horribly wrong with this scenario, and I pray that God remedies it in an expedient fashion.

The time has come for God's elders to step up to the plate and make the tough decisions that they were set apart to make. God does everything for a reason, and it may just be that God has appointed his elders of today for the explicit purpose of realigning God's resources with the biblical prescriptions. The stain being left by the modern approach to missionary support may yet still be wiped away. The time has not yet passed. For Christ's sake, may today's elders do what needs to be done and find great reward in heaven.

six

Where Is the Missionary to Go?

HAVING ESTABLISHED THE REALITY that God indeed has an eternal plan to gather his elect from among all the peoples of the earth and that missionaries are to be ordained by the church and sent throughout the world to preach the gospel, a very important question must now be asked. Where are these elect who are yet to be gathered? In other words, where is the missionary to go? Various passages have been considered that refer to the ends of the earth and nations and peoples, but what do these terms and phrases mean? What is meant in Genesis 12:3 by "all the families of the earth"? What is meant in Matthew 28:19 by "all nations"? What is meant by "the remotest part of the earth" in Acts 1:8? What is meant by "every tribe and tongue and people and nation" in Revelation 5:9? Do these terms and phrases refer to different ideas, or are they various ways of describing the same idea? The answer to this question is vital to the fulfillment of the church's role in the Great Enterprise, for only when the gospel has been preached in the whole world as a testimony to the nations will the end come (viz., Matt 24:14).

Before continuing on to answer the question at hand, another point must be made. The focus of this book is the ingathering of God's elect from among the nations. Therefore, I speak in terms of finding God's elect who are scattered abroad over the face of the whole earth. That does not mean, however, that there are not elect still waiting to hear the gospel and experience regeneration within areas that are considered to be reached by the gospel. There are, hopefully, millions of God's children who will soon hear the word of Christ in the United States, South Korea, Australia, Sub-Saharan Africa, and all the other areas where the gospel already flourishes. While preaching the gospel in these areas is essential, it is the job of the evangelist, as opposed to the job of the missionary, so the reader ought not get the notion that there is not anyone left in these areas who is still waiting to hear the gospel. There will always be people to whom the gospel must be preached, but the focus herein is the role of the missionary. To this, we now turn.

People Groups

By the middle of the twentieth century, every political nation in the world had been penetrated with the gospel. No doubt, this was an amazing feat wrought through the hard work, dedication, and sacrifice of many churches and their missionaries. This achievement, however, carried with it a false sense of success, and the veil that had drifted down over everyone's eyes was thrown off at the Lausanne International Consultation in 1974. This consultation was part of the First Lausanne Congress, in which 2,700 participants and guests from over 150 nations gathered in Lausanne, Switzerland for ten days of discussion, fellowship, worship, and prayer surrounding the issue of world evangelization. While some at the congress were calling for a cessation on foreign missions, Ralph Winter introduced the idea of "unreached people groups" during his plenary address and made the startling claim that nearly half of the world remained isolated from the gospel due to cultural, linguistic, and ethnic boundaries.[1]

While every political state in the world may have a functioning church within it, political states come and go and change and move. While the political nation of Brazil has a flourishing church, there is not a single believer within the Javae people of the Amazon. Were they to become their own political nation, suddenly not every nation in the world would have been penetrated with the gospel. Because of this, Winter argued that the term "nations" referred to in the Great Commission must mean something other than "political states." According to Winter, the biblical concept of "nations" really means "people groups."[2]

For a detailed and persuasive argument on this position, the reader should look at chapter 5 of John Piper's *Let the Nations Be Glad*. For the

---

1. "About," Lausanne Movement, para. 4–5.
2. "Our History," U.S. Center for World Mission, para. 2.

purposes herein, however, the following will suffice. The term "nations" does not refer to geopolitical entities. In other words, it does not refer to nations such as Australia or Germany. Geopolitical nations come and go. Their borders extend and retract. Their people migrate to and fro. Most important, geopolitical nations do not experience God's blessing as described in Genesis 12:3. Therefore, the term "nations" must refer to something more like the "Cherokee Nation" or a group of people linked together by ethnolinguistic similarities. The Greek word *ethnos* is translated into English as "nations" but is often translated as "Gentiles" and can mean a specific group of non-Jewish people or all non-Jewish people in general. In summary, Piper concludes that the English word "nations" is used in the New Testament to describe groups of people linked together by ethnolinguistic similarities.[3] Therefore, "nations" must mean something similar to "families of the earth"; for both are referring to groups of people linked together by blood, language, and/or culture. The only difference appears to be that of general description as opposed to a more specific description. "Nations" can refer to something as large as the Han people of China, while "families of the earth" may refer to something as small as the family of Jesse from the tribe of Judah. For the purposes herein, it is safe and accurate to assert that "nations" and "families of the earth" refer to the same idea but vary in terms of specificity.

Furthermore, there are three additional terms used in the biblical text that also refer to the same idea but vary in terms of specificity and the differing characteristics used to group *ethnos* together. Those terms are "people," "tribe," and "tongue." All of these terms are used in the various descriptions of God achieving the end for which he created the world through the blessing of the families of the earth as laid out in Genesis 12:1–3. That these additional terms refer to the same idea as "families of the earth" is clearly seen in that these terms are used to explain God's accomplishment of his chief end. This is found in Revelation 5:9, where the four living creatures and the twenty-four elders fell down before the Lamb and sang a new song, saying, "Worthy are You to take the book and to break its seals; for You were slain, and purchased for God with Your blood men from every tribe and tongue and people and nation." Here, it is seen that Christ was declared worthy because he has purchased for God, with his blood, men from among all the tribes, tongues, peoples,

---

3. Piper, *Let the Nations Be Glad*, 188.

and nations of the earth. God's ransom of his saints from among all the families of the earth is what portrays him as worthy. In other words, God's glory is displayed in his predestining, calling, justifying, and ultimately glorifying men from among all the nations or peoples of the earth. This is exactly the same thing that is stated in Genesis 12:1–3. The only difference is that Genesis 12:1–3 tells of God's promise to do it, and Revelation 5:9 tells of God's having done it.

Differing Views of People Groups

While the idea of "people groups" is now widely accepted among modern missionaries and mission agencies, there remains some disagreement as to how these various groups are to be classified and counted. In 2012, Joshua Project claimed there to be 16,788 people groups in the world,[4] while at the same time recognizing that other entities claimed there to be anywhere from ten thousand to nearly thirty thousand people groups.[5] Which is it? If there are elect within each group, how is the missionary to know how each group is defined?

Rather than cavil over the number of people groups and the manner in which they are categorized, it would behoove the church to recognize both the opacity of the biblical text and the distant reach of the promise in Genesis 12:3. What is known for sure is that not all the elect have been brought in from among the nations. If they had, the end would have come. Until Christ returns, the church can be sure that there remains work to be done. This very well may be the reason for the lack of definition concerning the term "nations" within the biblical text. If the boundary of every tribe and tongue and people and nation were known, it might lead to lethargy in the church. Without knowing exactly how much work is yet to be done, the church must strive forward. This is particularly true when the far-reaching promise of Genesis 12:3 is considered. All the families of the earth are to be blessed through Abraham. This surely does not refer to every covenant household, but it certainly refers to a comparatively small group of people in contrast to a geopolitical nation. Every family on the face of the earth will be reached with the gospel, and the elect of God within every family will be regenerated and brought into his everlasting

   4. "Great Commission Statistics," Joshua Project, line 1.
   5. "How Many People Groups Are There?" Joshua Project, lines 1–2.

kingdom with joy and praise. Regardless of how people groups are classified, there remains a great number of additional families within whom the elect are to be found.

Unreached People Groups

As various entities classify and count people groups, a very important category has emerged. This category contains those people groups that have yet to be reached with the gospel. Again, there are various ways to determine whether or not a people group has been reached with the gospel, but the statistics are quite staggering. According to Joshua Project, 6,951 of the 16,788 people groups have yet to be reached with the gospel as of 2012; and 41.6 percent of the world's population has remained among the people groups yet to be reached.[6] This means that nearly half of the world's population has been isolated from the gospel by cultural, linguistic, and ethnic boundaries. Thus, the only hope these people have of salvation is a missionary who crosses these cultural, linguistic, and ethnic boundaries in his endeavor to preach the gospel to the ends of the earth.

Amazing, also, is the geographic location of many of these peoples. Of Joshua Project's 6,951 unreached people groups in 2012, 5,887 of them resided in the 10/40 Window.[7] This geographic location runs from West Africa to East Asia and between 10 degrees north latitude and 40 degrees north latitude. The regions it includes are North Africa, the Middle East, Central and Southeast Asia, China, and Japan. These areas are dominated by Islam, Hinduism, Buddhism, and various animistic and tribal religions. Missionaries also find these areas some of the most difficult in which to live. Missionaries find it difficult to get into these areas for political reasons, and they find it difficult to stay for reasons ranging from cultural difficulties to persecution. The result is that these people groups have been widely neglected by the church's missionary activity. Churches tend to send missionaries to places perceived to be easier in which to live, and financial resources flow in the same direction. Given the reach of the biblical promise, this ought not be. The unreached people groups of the

---

6. "Great Commission Statistics," Joshua Project, lines 2–3.
7. "What is the 10/40 Window?" Joshua Project, para. 1.

10/40 Window, as well as those scattered through other parts of the globe, must be engaged with the gospel.

In order to make clear what has thus far only been referenced in terms of statistics, let me take the liberty of sharing some personal experiences. My first visit to Antakya, Turkey was in 2000. Antakya is located in the southern Hatay Province of Turkey, which was once part of Syria. During biblical times, the city was known as Syrian Antioch. As shown in earlier chapters, the church in Antioch was the sending entity for Paul and Barnabas. It was the place where the disciples were first called "Christians" (viz., Acts 11:26) and later became the See of the Gentile church. By the time I arrived in 2000, there were only ten known believers in the entire city. While the gospel had once flourished in Antioch, the invasion of Islam had literally eradicated the church for over one thousand years. For more than a millennium, the light of the gospel had been vanquished by the lie of Islam. The people of the city, and the entire region, were fettered in spiritual darkness apart from any hope of salvation. This remained so until the 1980s, when a Swedish missionary arrived in Antakya with the light of the gospel of the glory of God. In the two decades of ministry between his arrival and my first visit to Antakya, there were only a handful of God's elect found in the city; but there were, and still are, more to come. In the twelve years following my first visit, there were roughly one hundred children of God found in the city. The light of the gospel has begun to shine once again; and though the work is difficult, God's children are out there. They will return home with joy and praise when they hear the good news of the gospel.

A number of years ago, I met a missionary in central China. He was visiting villages in the area, trying to determine whether there were any indigenous churches already there; so he spent weeks traveling from village to village, asking people if they had ever heard of Jesus. He got the same response time after time. The people had no knowledge of the name of Jesus. The missionary thought he had found a glimmer of hope one day when he asked a man if he knew anything of Jesus. The man responded, "Yes." With hope growing in the missionary's heart, the man continued, "I think he lives in the next village." The man knew nothing of the Christ. He had only confused Jesus' name with that of someone in the next village. The missionary found no one in the entire region who had been exposed to the gospel.

It is an eerie thing for a missionary to walk down the street and know that every person he sees is fettered in spiritual chains without any hope of salvation. Most saints do not often think of the God-hating rebellion that dwells within the hearts of those around them or the dreadful yet just wrath of God that hangs over the heads of the reprobate. However, missionaries face it everyday, and Bible-saturated ambition compels them to rebuke such rebellion and proclaim amnesty in Christ. By the grace of God, these fettered people are broken free of their bonds and freed to seek everlasting joy in the praise of God.

I remember vividly the first time I shared the gospel in this kind of context. It was during a short visit to a country in the heart of the 10/40 Window. Having maneuvered my way into an English class as a guest speaker, I was able to make a few English-speaking friends. I took them out for dessert after class and began to share with them why I was there. I explained to them that I had been sent there to declare to them the way of salvation through Jesus Christ. I explained Christ's role as the Mediator between God and man and that the only hope of evading the wrath of God was to repent from rebellion and trust in the mercy of Christ. At that point, one of them stood up and had on his face a look that I had never seen before. It was a look of anxiety, bewilderment, excitement, and joy. Then, he said, "We have never heard anything like this before. This is amazing." Those who were appointed to eternal life believed that night and began to glorify the word of the Lord.

The statistics concerning unreached people groups are daunting, but they must not dissuade the church. God has made a habit of fulfilling his promises in the bleakest of times. Only in her old age did Sarah conceive and bear Isaac to Abraham. Isaac's own wife, Rebekah, was barren for twenty years before giving birth to Jacob. It was from the bonds of slavery that Israel was redeemed from Egypt. Only because of famine did a barren and widowed Moabitess named Ruth become the mother of David's grandfather. God himself came to earth as a human infant, the weakest and most vulnerable of all creatures. When the task appears most difficult, that is generally when God gives success.

The Great Enterprise from a Reformed Perspective

Determining Where the Missionary Is to Go

With the daunting task laid before the church and success guaranteed, where is the missionary to go? When answering this question, churches clearly need to take into account the scope of the biblical promise and the reality of the existence of unreached peoples today. These peoples ought to be the priority, but there are other factors that must be considered as well. Other factors that may very well prevent the missionary from engaging these unreached peoples will be considered here first, followed by an exhortation to reach the unreached.

The missionary may have other responsibilities that trump missionary activity. This is particularly true for the married missionary. Paul accurately observes in 1 Corinthians that the married man is concerned with the things of the world, namely, how to please his wife (viz., 1 Cor 7:33). The married missionary has as his first responsibility the cleansing and sanctifying of his wife by the washing of water with the word (viz., Eph 5:26) and the training of his children, if he has any, in the way of the Lord (viz., Prov 22:6). The married missionary is charged with ensuring that his family is cared for spiritually and also physically (viz., 2 Thess 3:12). The missionary should not embark upon anything that would prevent him from fulfilling his responsibilities. For a married father to walk across the boarder from China to North Korea with a backpack full of Bibles would not be wise or prudent. The almost certain outcome would be his immediate imprisonment, leaving him unable to care and provide for his family. A single man with no one under his care is free to do as he pleases, and maybe he could have a fruitful prison ministry in North Korea. However, the married missionary has other responsibilities that he must consider first.

There are two pitfalls in this area that should be highlighted. The first one discourages the missionary from venturing to the ends of the earth, and the second one discourages the missionary from fulfilling his responsibilities in the home. As for the former, mission agencies and churches too often presume to know how a man ought to best care for his family. Say, for instance, a missionary's son has a particular medical condition, which requires particular medical care. Churches and agencies may want to dictate where this missionary can serve based upon their knowledge of the medical condition and its unique requirements. However, the husband is the head of the family (viz., Eph 5:23) and is ultimately responsible for the family's well-being. Churches and agencies can and should provide counsel, but the final decision must remain with the missionary. No one is to tell him in which geographic locations he ought to raise his family. So, the missionary is to be counseled but is not to be stopped in his missionary efforts on account of outside perceptions of his family's potential well-being.

As to the latter, there is too often a perception in the mission field that missionary activity ought to be the top priority for the missionary. Some missionaries have the false notion that if they take care of the ministry, God will take care of their families. This is an outright rejection of what Scripture teaches. Men are given to their families for the specific purpose of taking care of them. The thought that this somehow does not apply to missionaries is absurd. While missionary activity is of incredible significance, it is not more important than the family. William Carey is rightly characterized as the father of the modern missionary movement and credited with bringing the gospel to India, but his neglect of his family is often overlooked. Carey's wife, Dorothy, was physically confined to her room with madness for twelve years as a result of the inability to cope mentally and emotionally with the difficulties of missionary life in India.[8] She could have suffered such a breakdown at home in England, but it was Carey's failure to help her manage that reflected poorly on his execution of his family responsibilities. Carey's primary responsibility ought to have been the spiritual well-being of his wife, yet she almost completely vanished from Carey's life after she was diagnosed with mental illness.[9] God certainly used Carey, but that was no excuse for the neglect of his family. No missionary should be dissuaded from caring for his family, either by blinding ambition for missionary service or by outside criticism from others who are so blinded. Even in the mission field, the married missionary's family ought to be his top priority.

Assuming he has tended to his other responsibilities, the missionary ought to look to unreached peoples. Joshua Project is an outstanding resource for anyone seeking detailed information on unreached people groups. However, there is no biblical formula for determining where the missionary is to go. Paul's ambition was to preach the gospel in Spain because he desired to preach where the gospel had not yet been heard, but

---

8. Walker, *William Carey*, 250.
9. Drewery, *William Carey*, 82–83.

there were plenty of areas that had yet to be reached by the gospel. Why did Paul not desire to preach the gospel to Germanic tribes in northern Europe? Why did he not desire to preach the gospel to the Berber tribes of Morocco? The biblical text does not answer these questions. All that is said is that Paul desired to preach the gospel where it had not yet been preached, and the text lists one of those areas. The conclusion, therefore, ought to be that any such area is an acceptable place for a missionary to go. There is personal freedom in determining on which unreached areas the missionary should focus. It is entirely possible that Paul had wanted to visit Spain ever since he was a child, and he united his desire to see Spain with his desire to preach the gospel. This is pure speculation, but it would be perfectly acceptable if it were true. The decision to target any unreached people group is a good and biblically acceptable decision.

With that said, the missionary and his sending church ought to consider his and his family's adaptability to certain cultures when determining where the missionary ought to be sent. If he hates lamb and falafel but loves rice and noodles, he may consider taking the gospel to central China as opposed to the Middle East. If he and his family have some strange desire to live in a tent, he may want to consider bringing the gospel to the Bedouin tribes of Jordan or Egypt. If he and his family love metropolitan cities, he may want to consider bringing the gospel to Tokyo. If he and his family are prone to making breathy and guttural sounds when they speak, he may want to consider bringing the gospel to Arabic-speaking people. There are a host of legitimate factors that can point the missionary in a particular direction. So long as the focus is preaching the gospel to unreached peoples, there is great freedom in determining the best course of action.

Final Exhortation

While there is freedom in determining which unreached people group to target, the church and her missionaries are not free to ignore unreached people groups. God has sent certain people, at particular times, to serve in the cause of the gospel in areas where the church was well established. Timothy was an excellent example of this. He was from the area of Derby and Lystra, but Paul sent him to the Ephesian church to do the work of an evangelist. This, however, is the exception and not the rule. The rule for the missionary is to push "to the remotest part of the earth" (Acts 1:8). Therefore, the church ought to reallocate most of its missionary resources, both human and financial, to unreached areas. The Great Enterprise is not about perpetuating the church in the areas where it is established. Rather, it is about finding and gathering together all of God's children who are scattered over the face of the whole earth. The culmination of the Great Enterprise will not come to fruition without the church turning its focus to unreached people groups. Due to God's faithfulness, this will happen; but the sooner it happens, the better off the church will be both now and forever. Remember, no one outside of Judea, including the reader of this book, would have any hope of salvation apart from missionary activity. Any believer who is not a Jew from Judea has the efforts of missionaries to thank for having heard the gospel. Let nothing, then, prevent the church from continuing this great heritage and gathering together all of the elect so that they all with one voice may proclaim, "Great is the LORD and greatly to be praised" (Psalm 96:4).

seven

The Missionary's Preaching

THIS CHAPTER ADDRESSES TWO interrelated aspects of missionary ministry, namely, the act of preaching the gospel and to whom it is to be preached. The previous chapter addressed the issue of where the missionary is to be sent. That is not what is meant here. Rather, through consideration of Christ's instructions in Matthew 10, this chapter considers which individuals within unreached people groups are to receive the gospel. First, however, we will consider that which the missionary is to preach.

The Gospel

This was hinted at in previous chapters, but the pitifully unfortunate truncation of the gospel into social services must be stated again. Suppose a child suffering from a painful disease visits a doctor. Even though he has the cure for this disease in his office, the doctor only prescribes a regimen of pain relievers, not wanting to frighten the child regarding the severity of his condition. No one would call this love. In fact, this would be seen more as some twisted form of torture than love, but this happens regularly within modern missionary activity. Missionaries go out into the world with the cure for sin and wrath in their back pocket, but they only offer temporary pain relievers. That this could possibly be seen as pleasing in God's eyes is nonsense. Providing physical aid without prescribing the gospel is a terrible thing to do. Attributed to St. Francis of Assisi is the saying, "Preach the gospel always; and when necessary, use words." Intimated in this quote is that it is not always necessary to preach the gospel with words, that people will somehow be loved to the cross. Such

The Missionary's Preaching

an approach is an abandonment of the gospel and an outright rejection of Paul's words in 2 Timothy 1:8, where he says, "Therefore do not be ashamed of the testimony of our Lord." What follows in this section is a survey of what the gospel actually is.

The term "gospel" is used ninety-five times in the New Testament, and it simply means "good news." So, there are two components to the term. First, the gospel is good. Second, the gospel is news, indicating it was once previously unknown. What is it about the gospel that makes it good, and in what way was it previously unknown? It is to these questions that we now turn.

Too often, the gospel is boiled down to historical events, and acceptance of the gospel is boiled down to acceptance of the reality of those historical events. This, however, is insufficient. When the southern states seceded from the Union in 1861 and formed the Confederate States of America, the Union recognized that these events had happened, but the Union was in disagreement with design behind these events. The same can be true in regards to the gospel. An individual can accept the historical facts of the life, death, and resurrection of Jesus Christ but remain in opposition to the design of these events or the purpose for which they took place. A question must now be asked. What is the design of the gospel? In other words, why did God cause the historical events of the gospel to take place?

By now, the reader should see clearly that God's aim or purpose in everything is to glorify and magnify himself. This is also true in his design of the gospel. This is seen in John 12:23, where Jesus said in reference to his crucifixion, "The hour has come for the Son of Man to be glorified." The central event of the gospel has as its purpose the glorification of Jesus Christ. Therefore, the display of the glory of God is central to the gospel, and no one can accept the gospel without embracing its design of displaying God's glory. According to Piper, "If you embrace the facets of the gospel, but do it in a way that does not make the glory of God in Christ your supreme treasure, then you have not embraced the gospel."[1] The unfortunate reality is that many people within the modern church have embraced the historical facets of the gospel but still lack the glory of God, and many missionaries preach the historical facets of the gospel but neglect to proclaim its purpose.

---

1. Piper, *God Is the Gospel*, 35.

There is another question that logically follows. If the design of the gospel, which is to display the glory of God, must be accepted along with the gospel's historical events, what then is the glory of God? In the English language, "glory" is an interesting word often associated with sporting events. Merriam-Webster defines "glory" as "something that secures praise or renown."[2] This definition fits with the term's use in sport. The glory that comes with winning a championship is that which secures praise and renown. A football team being crowned champion secures praise and renown because the team has, through victory on the field, demonstrated its praiseworthy ability. The same thing is true of the gospel. Christ referred to his crucifixion as glorification because it demonstrated his praiseworthy ability and secured praise and renown for eternity. The glory of God, therefore, is the display of God's magnificent ability. Creation is a prime example of this. Psalm 8:3 refers to the heavens as "the work of [God's] fingers." The heavens formed in Genesis 1 are the work of God's fingers. The stars of the sky are a dazzling display of the magnificent ability of God, but there is yet a greater display. While creation brilliantly displays the ability of God, it does not display his greatest ability, nor does it display the person for whom it ought to secure praise and renown. This is what makes the gospel necessary. Only in the gospel is God's greatest ability shown along with the person for whom it secures praise and renown.

The gospel clearly declares Jesus Christ as the one to whom praise is due. Hebrews 1:6 states that even "all the angels of God worship Him." While the stars do not declare the particular entity to whom praise is due, the gospel does. Jude says, "To the only God our Savior, through Jesus Christ our Lord, be glory, majesty, dominion and authority, before all time and now and forever. Amen" (Jude 1:25). That the gospel could be preached or somehow lived without demanding the creature's praise of the glory of Christ is ridiculous. It would be like a mountain climber seeking to climb to the top of Mount Everest without reaching the summit. Reaching the summit is the whole point of climbing to the top, and it is not possible to climb to the top without reaching the summit. The gospel without the glory of Christ would be just as absurd.

As for the greatest ability of God, it is displayed in the gospel. Creation and the various miracles recorded in Scripture are astonishing

---

2. *Merriam-Webster's Collegiate Dictionary*, 10th ed., s.v. "glory."

displays of divine ability. Has anyone other than God commanded the morning (viz., Job 38:12)? Does anyone other than God hold the breath of mankind and the life of every living thing in the palm of his hand (viz., Job 12:10)? Did anyone else split the Red Sea and cause Israel to walk on dry land (viz., Exod 14:21–22)? Has anyone other than Jesus given sight to a man blind from birth (viz., John 9:1)? While these are displays of glory beyond which any mere man could perform, they pale in comparison to the display of the glory of God's grace on the cross.

The state of the natural human condition is one in which "there is no fear of God" (Rom 3:18). No natural man understands or seeks God, and all have turned aside and become useless (viz., Rom 3:10–12). No natural man has faith (viz., Eph 2:8), and he displeases God continuously (viz., Heb 11:6) by committing idolatry in his seeking pleasure in created things rather than in the Creator of all things (viz., Rom 1:23). Yet, it is from natural men that God seeks to secure praise and renown. Everyone born of Adam is born with an innate hatred for God, yet the Scriptures boldly claim that "all the ends of the earth will remember and turn to the LORD, And all the families of the nations will worship before" him (Ps 22:27). How can this be? The earth is filled with God-hating sinners, and God thinks that all the nations are going to worship him. Creating and naming the stars (viz., Ps 147:4) is one thing. Securing worship from those who hate him is another.

Something must happen to the natural man in order for him to worship God. To worship God would be pleasing to him, meaning, that one must first have faith before ascribing worth to God through pleasing worship (viz., Heb 11:6). In order for someone to have faith and believe that Jesus is the Christ, faith must first be granted to the person by God (viz., Eph 2:8). In order for one to believe that Jesus is the Christ, he must be born of God (viz., 1 John 5:1). Jesus said in John 3:3, "Truly, truly, I say to you, unless one is born again he cannot see the kingdom of God." This intimates that being born again is what allows a man to believe, have faith, and ascribe worship. The miracle of rebirth, therefore, is that which must happen to the natural man in order for him to worship God. This is the first component of the display of God's greatest ability. The Spirit blows where he wishes and begets spirit within whom he wishes (viz., John 3:6, 8). Regeneration by the Holy Spirit is what allows a man to see the kingdom of God and is part of the display of God's greatest ability, but it is not part of the visible display. Rather, it is what allows the visible display to be seen. Through regeneration, Christ provides the spiritual eye salve to the one regenerated so that spiritual eyes can see spiritual things (viz., Rev 3:18).

Giving men eyes to see and causing them to be reborn (viz., 1 Pet 1:3) is only part of the process, for there must be something for these eyes to behold. Someone with reading glasses does not praise the manufacturer of his eyeglasses when he reads the newspaper in the morning. He simply reads and enjoys the newspaper. If God were to give eyes to see but not provide the thing to be seen, he would not secure for himself praise and renown. He would simply be a means to a different end. Therefore, God must not only supply sight through regeneration but must also provide that which is to be seen, and that which is to be seen is the glory of his grace.

It is no coincidence that, in John 3, Jesus went straight from teaching the doctrine of regeneration to saying that men must look upon him crucified in order to have eternal life. Regeneration leads immediately to seeing the glory of God. Paul makes this clear in 2 Corinthians 4:6, saying, "For God, who said, 'Light shall shine out of darkness,' is the One who has shown in our hearts to give the Light of the knowledge of the glory of God in the face of Christ." In this verse is regeneration through the shining of light into the heart of man and man's receiving sight and beholding the glory of God in Christ—both of which result in the praise of the glory of God's grace (viz., Eph 1:6). This process is the greatest ability of God and is the message of the gospel.

The gospel is the power of God unto salvation (viz., Rom 1:16), because it is both the cause of regeneration and also that which regeneration allows man to see. Romans 10 tells of this beautiful process in an inverted fashion. Paul begins by speaking of salvation in Romans 10:13 and ends by speaking of regeneration in Romans 10:17. In reverse, these verses go as follows. Christ speaks, which causes hearing (viz., v. 17). This is an analogy describing regeneration, similar to Paul saying in 2 Corinthians 4:6 that God has shone into the saint's heart to give the light of the knowledge of the glory of God. Christ speaks through the preaching of the gospel (viz., v. 15), which allows the gospel to be heard and faith to be received (viz., v. 17). Hearing the gospel allows belief in Christ, and belief in Christ allows his name to be called upon (viz., v. 14). Calling upon the

The Missionary's Preaching

name of Christ brings about salvation (viz., v. 13), and the entire process secures praise and renown for God.

So, regeneration happens through the preaching of the gospel, but what is it exactly that regeneration allows to be seen? What is it that the natural man cannot see but that the regenerate man can see? According to John 3:14–15, seeing Christ lifted up, as Moses lifted the serpent in the wilderness, is what the physical eye is to gaze upon, but what is it in the slaughter of Christ on the cross that regenerate men see but that natural men are unable to see? Paul answers this question in 1 Corinthians 1:18, saying, "For the word of the cross is foolishness to those who are perishing, but to us who are being saved it is the power of God." When the natural man looks upon the cross, he sees foolishness. Only a fool would die in the place of guilty sinners. One will hardly die for a righteous man; but in order to demonstrate his love, Christ died for sinners (viz., Rom 5:7–8). This is totally contrary to the way the natural man thinks. The natural man would receive someone coming in his own name seeking his own glory (viz., John 5:43). The natural man seeks glory from men and is, therefore, unable to believe (viz., John 5:44). The thought of God giving up his glory (viz., Phil 2:6) for the sake of sinners looks like foolishness to the natural man. "After all, how could Jesus being nailed to a piece of lumber on a remote hill in a barren part of the world ages ago have any possible relevance to modern humanity or eternal destiny?"[3] The wisdom of the world denounces the cross as nonsense.

Furthermore, there are religions that accept some of the historical events of the gospel but that still manage to reject the cross. Islam teaches that Jesus was born of a virgin and lived a sinless life. Muslims also believe that someone thought to be Jesus died on a cross. However, Allah would never allow such a good man to suffer such an awful death, so Allah took Jesus up to heaven prior to being nailed to the cross and replaced Jesus with a stunt-double. Even though they reject the deity of Christ, Muslims still cannot fathom anything but foolishness in the idea of the cross.

Do Islam and the wisdom of the world have a case? Is the cross foolishness? According to John MacArthur, Paul never even tried to convince the Corinthian church that the gospel should be seen as wise in the eyes of the world but instead "conceded that the gospel is utter foolishness in

---

3. MacArthur, *Ashamed of the Gospel*, 111.

the eyes of human wisdom."[4] Conceding this point, Paul goes on in 1 Corinthians 1:25, saying, "The foolishness of God is wiser than men, and the weakness of God is stronger than men." Though it is odd to even speak of the foolishness of God, Paul's point is that what appears like God acting foolishly is infinitely wiser than what natural men can conceive. This "does not demonstrate any defect in the gospel. Rather, it underscores the deficiency of human wisdom."[5]

So, in a natural and humanistic sense, the gospel is foolishness, but the gospel was designed in divine wisdom. In other words, natural eyes see a man hanging on a tree and rightly count what they see as foolishness, but spiritual eyes see the wrath of God poured out on the Son of Man as substitutionary atonement in the place of his posterity and rightly count what they see as joyous salvation. What the natural man sees is indeed foolishness, and what the regenerate man sees is indeed the power of God for salvation. For those with eyes to see, the gospel message displays God's eternal plan to redeem guilty sinners through the life, death, and resurrection of the Mediator, thus securing their worship of him by demonstrating and making visible his glory and renown. It is no use to tell a blind man of the beauty of the ocean unless in his being told of this beauty, he gains the ability to see the beauty of the ocean. This is what the gospel does. The message itself proclaims aloud the greatest display of the glory of God and provides the hearer with the ability to behold the wondrous display of the cross.

Before moving on from this section, it is important to state clearly what the gospel message proclaims. Confusion in this matter is unacceptable, for the gospel message itself is essential to the fulfillment of the Great Enterprise. In Romans 3:24–26, Paul clearly states what took place on the cross and why. Christ Jesus was displayed publicly. This was not the prophet Isa of Islam. This was not the created Jesus of the Church of Jesus Christ of Latter-day Saints or of Jehovah's Witnesses. This was the Son of Man from Daniel 7:13–14, who "came up to the Ancient of Days And was presented before Him. And to Him was given dominion, Glory and a kingdom, That all the peoples, nations and men of every language Might serve Him." This was he who "is the radiance of [God's] glory and the exact representation of His nature, and [who] upholds all things by the

---

4. Ibid, 108.
5. Ibid, 107.

The Missionary's Preaching

word of His power" (Heb 1:3). This was the one whose glory was revealed to Isaiah, causing the thresholds of the foundations to tremble (viz., Isa 6:1–6; John 12:38). This was he whom God made both Lord and Christ, Jesus who was crucified (viz., Acts 2:36). Christ Jesus, who was and is God incarnate, was displayed publicly on the cross.

Continuing in Romans 3, God publicly displayed Christ Jesus on the cross as a propitiation, which was an appeasement of the wrath of God and which served to demonstrate the righteousness of God, for "in the forbearance of God He passed over the sins previously committed" (v. 25). Prior to the cross, God had passed over sins for millennia. God claims to be justified when he speaks and blameless when he judges (viz., Ps 51:4); yet he has passed over an uncountable number of sins, not the least of which were rape and murder (viz., 2 Sam 12:13). Passing over sin is not just, and letting people live who should die is not blameless. So, there is a problem that must be dealt with. God aims to secure glory and renown, but he appears to be a fraud. Again, this is foolishness to the world, but divine wisdom deliberately planned to demonstrate "His righteousness at [that] present time, so that He would be just and the justifier of the one who has faith in Jesus" (Rom 3:26). In order to demonstrate his righteous judgments while passing over sins, God publicly displayed the outpouring of his wrath on the Son of Man, leaving no doubt as to his blameless nature. Furthermore, God not only revealed himself as just but also as the justifier through suffering wrath in the place of those who put their faith in Christ. This great exchange is the greatest of God's accomplishments. The law-fulfilling Christ who knew no sin was made to be sin on behalf of his posterity, while at the same time imputing his own righteousness to them (viz., 2 Cor 5:21). In this exchange, God displayed his own righteousness and secured for himself glory and renown by demonstrating his praiseworthy ability to be both just and the justifier.

Only those with spiritual eyes can see this; but when they do, they both rejoice and lament. They rejoice because it is the best news ever to be heard. The wrath of God has been exhausted and eternal life secured. How could that not bring exultation? Lamentation, however, follows as well, for the gospel reveals the true nature of every man by publicly displaying that which every man deserves. Not only that, the gospel displays the innocent Christ suffering the wrath of God in the place of men.

The Great Enterprise from a Reformed Perspective

When spiritual eyes see this, tears of sorrow and regret come pouring out. After telling the Jews that they had killed the Christ in Acts 2:36, Peter commanded them to repent in verse 38. The gospel must be preached in such a way that demonstrates God as both just and the justifier. This means that the message must contain the wrath of God and man's need for atonement and justification. Any gospel message that does not proclaim God as wrathful and just and man as sinful is no gospel message at all. When the regenerate man receives the gospel, it will bring him to his knees in lament-filled confession and cause him to look heavenward in exultation over the exaltation of the glory of God in the face of Christ. If this is not reflective of a man's reception of the gospel, then he has not received the gospel.

There is yet one more point that must be made. Though hinted at in the previous paragraph, it must be made explicit. Exulting over the exaltation of the glory of God in the face of Christ is necessary evidence of regeneration and faith in Christ, for eternal life consists of knowing God (viz., John 17:3). Eternal life does not consist merely of being forgiven and escaping the wrath of God. Unregenerate men, at times, seek forgiveness and desire to avoid the wrath of God. In the words of Piper, "It doesn't take a new heart to want the psychological relief of forgiveness, or the removal of God's wrath, or the inheritance of God's world. You don't need to be born again to want these things. The evidence that we have been changed is that we want these things because they bring us to the enjoyment of God."[6] Remember the point made in chapter 1 regarding Ephesians 1:3–6, that God designed the eternal covenant before anything else even existed so that he could enjoy seeing the glory of his grace. If prior to the creation of the universe God had designed the demonstration of his righteousness and justification of his people in the cross so that he could enjoy beholding his own ability, it certainly follows that his people ought now to enjoy beholding that same ability. A question was asked at the beginning of this section; what is it about the gospel that makes it good? The gift of the glory of God is what makes the gospel good. The gospel portrays God as the ultimate source of supreme joy and frees the hearer to enjoy God for all eternity. The gift of God in the gospel is what makes it good. In the words of David, "As for me, I shall behold Your face in righteousness; I will be satisfied with Your likeness when I awake" (Ps

---

6. Piper, *God Is the Gospel*, 35.

17:15). The gospel satisfies because it is the gift of beholding God's face and being acquainted with his likeness.

Now, a second question was asked at the beginning of this section; namely, in what way was the gospel previously unknown? If the gospel is good because it gives God for the enjoyment of the hearer, in what way is the gospel news? There are two ways in which the gospel is news. The first way has been hinted at already. That is, all men are spiritually dead prior to the miracle of regeneration, meaning, that it is impossible for anyone to comprehend the message of the gospel prior to regeneration. Even though a person may have heard the message numerous times in an unregenerate state, the gospel becomes news the first time it is heard with the proper spiritual ears. This is the case for every saint who hears Christ's effectual call through the proclamation of the gospel. This is one way in which the gospel is news.

There is also a second way in which the gospel is news. Paul says in Ephesians 3:4-5 that the mystery of Christ was not made known to the sons of men in other generations. This mystery, to be specific, is that "the Gentiles are fellow heirs and fellow members of the body, and fellow partakers of the promise in Christ Jesus through the gospel" (Eph 3:6). God has hidden this mystery for ages; but now, the manifold wisdom of God is being revealed through the church (viz., Eph 3:9-10). There was a time when the God of Abraham, Isaac, and Jacob was thought to be a tribal deity. There was a time when the nations had no portion in the promises made to Abraham; but now, according to the "gospel and the preaching of Jesus Christ, according to the revelation of the mystery which has been kept secret for long ages past, but now is manifested, and by the Scriptures of the prophets, according to the commandment of the eternal God" (Rom 16:25-26), all the families of the earth shall be blessed through the seed of Abraham, who is Jesus Christ (viz., Gal 3:16).

Therefore, the gospel is the good news that God is indeed both just and the justifier of those who place their faith in Christ and that these promises extend to all the families of the earth. Amnesty and eternal life are offered to those who deserve judgment and eternal wrath. There is now a path to find ultimate joy in the worship of he who has secured infinite glory and renown through the demonstration of his divine and praiseworthy ability. This is the gospel message, and it must not be compromised. The missionary is to boldly and unashamedly proclaim these things to the nations. This is not a message that is true for some and not for others. The nations must be commanded to worship Christ regardless of their cultural and religious differences with the gospel. The warning of Lesslie Newbigin ought to be heeded. He says in his book *The Gospel in a Pluralist Society*, "The relativism which is not willing to speak about truth but only about 'what is true for me' is an evasion of the serious business of living. It is the mark of a tragic loss of nerve in our contemporary culture. It is a preliminary symptom of death."[7] These are tough but warranted words. Proclaiming the gospel as anything other than absolute truth for all people of all ages is a sign of death in the church.

Charles Spurgeon saw these signs during what is known as the "downgrade controversy." According to MacArthur, Spurgeon argued with the Baptist Union that "biblical truth is like the pinnacle of a steep, slippery mountain. One step away, and you find yourself on the downgrade."[8] This is why the gospel message must not be compromised. One step away from the pinnacle of biblical truth leads to death. Even if it is unpopular or unwelcome, the missionary must remain true to all the facets of the gospel and continually proclaim the full and unadulterated message of the cross.

This leads to the second section of this chapter. If the missionary is to continually proclaim the full and unadulterated message of the cross, is he to continually proclaim it to people who reject it? In other words, how is the missionary to know which individuals to preach to within unreached people groups? It is to this question that we now turn.

To Whom Shall the Missionary Preach?

When the missionary first arrives among an unreached people, he should seek to preach the gospel to anyone and everyone to whom he is able to preach. It should be noted that it is up to the missionary to determine who these individuals are and that his ability to preach is very often dependent upon the cultural and political atmosphere in which he finds himself. There are some villages in Southeast Asia where missionaries seek out

---

7. Newbigin, *The Gospel in a Pluralist Society*, 22.
8. MacArthur, *Ashamed of the Gospel*, 21.

the village chief and explain the gospel to him. If he responds favorably, the whole village comes and receives Christ. In Afghanistan, a missionary would probably be executed for publicly seeking out the village leader with the gospel. These kinds of things must be taken into consideration, and only the missionary is able to make the proper determination.

Once the missionary determines to whom he is able to preach, he should do so. Whether it happens during the course of six months over coffee or during one afternoon in a public square is immaterial. He should preach, and those appointed to eternal life will believe (viz., Acts 13:48). While regeneration, or at least its evidence, is not always instantaneous, the missionary must distinguish between those interested in the gospel and those who see it as foolishness. Christ's instructions were quite clear in Matthew 10:14, where he said, "Whoever does not receive you, nor heed your words, as you go out of that house or that city, shake the dust off your feet." Christ spoke similarly in Matthew 7:6, saying, "Do not give what is holy to dogs, and do not throw your pearls before swine, or they will trample them under their feet, and turn and tear you to pieces." This is a stern warning to not waste the gospel message on those who will tear the missionary to pieces on account of it. However, the missionary must at least begin preaching to these people in order to know how they will respond.

When the hearers respond negatively, the missionary is to wipe the dust off of his feet in order that he may deliver pearls to the elect who are still waiting for the gospel. This is precisely what Paul did in Acts 13. Paul began preaching to the Jews, but "when the Jews saw the crowds, they were filled with jealousy and began contradicting the things spoken by Paul, and were blaspheming" (Acts 13:45). At that point, Paul turned and preached to the Gentiles, and "as many as had been appointed to eternal life believed" (Acts 13:48). Two things should be noted here. First, Paul preached to the Jews. He preached to those who would reject the gospel. Second, he shook the dust off his feet (viz., Acts 13:51) and delivered pearls to those appointed to eternal life. The missionary of today must do the same thing. He must preach even to those who may ridicule and persecute him for it. This was Paul's custom everywhere he went. He always preached to the Jews, knowing the likelihood of their rejection of the gospel message, but he never hesitated to turn from them and let them wallow in their own blindness once their rejection of the gospel was evident. Again, the missionary of today must be willing to preach to the hardest of people but not continue to waste the word of the cross on those who see it as foolishness.

A word of caution must be advised here, for not seeing the gospel clearly is not the same as seeing it as foolishness. This is where the missionary must distinguish between those interested in the gospel and those who see it as foolishness. When a child is born, he can see very little. He has never seen anything other than darkness, and the bright lights of the hospital can be quite confusing. The same is true of a man awakened from a deep sleep in the middle of the night. Sometimes, he may not even know where he is, much less be able to make out distinct characters on the other side of the room. The same principle applies to those born of and awakened by the Spirit. They have never used their spiritual eyes before. Some facets of the gospel may still appear fuzzy and undistinguishable to them. This must not be confused with their seeing the gospel as foolishness. These people are just beginning to see the divine wisdom of the cross, and their new eyes must be given time to focus. This does not mean, though, that the missionary should water down the message. In fact, it means just the opposite. The missionary ought to make his message as offensive to the natural man as possible. This will help newly formed spiritual eyes to focus and also reveal those whose god is still their appetite (viz., Phil 3:19).

Final Thoughts

The St. Francis of Assisi quote stated earlier should be augmented to read, "Preach the gospel always; and when necessary, shake the dust off your feet and go elsewhere." The missionary must always seek to preach the full and unadulterated word of the cross, but he must not throw his pearls before swine. Missionaries are a fragrant aroma of Christ to God, and this aroma smells like death among those who are perishing and like life among those who are being saved (viz., 2 Cor 2:15). Those who smell death must be left to die, and those who smell life must be given the pearls of the gospel, for God is glorified in both his just wrath and his abundant grace.

There is no other option for the missionary. As John Calvin says, "When duly imbued with the knowledge of him, the whole aim of our lives will be to revere, fear, and worship his majesty, to acknowledge, loud,

The Missionary's Preaching

and celebrate the magnificence of his works, to make him, as it were, the sole aim of all our actions."⁹ There is no room here for compromise. There is no place in the church or in the mission field for variations of the gospel. As the aim of his life, the missionary is to preach one gospel that brings death and condemnation to some and justification and eternal life to others.

---

9. Calvin, *Institutes of the Christian Religion*, 242–3.

eight

The Missionary's Teaching

THIS CHAPTER IS ESSENTIALLY an exposition of the phrase, "teaching them to observe all that I commanded you" (Matt 28:20). Christ followed his command to go and make disciples of all the nations with two phrases that were descriptive of the process of making disciples. The apostles were to make disciples of all the nations by baptizing them in the name of the Father and the Son and the Holy Spirit and by teaching them to obey all that Christ had commanded. The first descriptive phrase is fairly straightforward. For both pedobaptists and credobaptists, baptism is the physical sign of entrance into the church. Therefore, the missionary is to bring all converts into the church through the physical sign of baptism. Under pedobaptist doctrine, descendants of believers have the right to be brought into God's visible covenant people as well. It is not the aim of this chapter or of this book, however, to deal with the differences between pedobaptism and credobaptism. Rather than discussing the mode of baptism and to whom it should be administered, the point here is that those who respond to the gospel in faith are to be brought into the church. As for the second descriptive phrase, teaching the nations to obey all that Christ commanded is much more in-depth and complex. This chapter, therefore, is a survey of the essential commandments of Christ that the missionary must teach the nations to obey.

Christ and the Law and the Prophets

Of utmost importance is the relationship between Christ's teaching and the teaching of the Old Testament. Jesus said that the Old Testament

The Missionary's Teaching

Scriptures pointed to and spoke of him (viz., John 5:39) and that he did not come to abolish the law but to fulfill it (viz., Matt 5:17). This means that Christ did not add anything to the essential teachings of orthodoxy but rather confirmed the doctrines of the Old Testament and fulfilled that which was spoken of him. The moral law of God is to be obeyed today just as it was prior to the advent of Christ, and Jesus' ministry and teaching served to demonstrate that he was indeed the Messiah spoken of in the Old Testament. To these two areas of teaching we now turn, beginning with God's moral law and then Christ's teaching—namely, that which he taught regarding himself.

The Moral Law

A brief point must now be made regarding what is meant by "moral law." Within the Reformed tradition, this phrase refers to that part of the Mosaic law that is perpetual and immutable in that it is a reflection of God's perfect and unchanging character. For example, God's law forbids murder. This was true prior to the Exodus, during the Mosaic economy, and it remains true today. Murder is contrary to God's perfect and immutable character. Therefore, the prohibition against murder is a perpetual law or a moral law of God. The moral law has been in effect since the beginning of time and will remain in effect perpetually.

This is in contrast to the other parts of the Mosaic law—namely, the ceremonial law and civil law. The ceremonial law dealt with the manner in which the Israelites were to approach God through temple worship, and it contained a long list of elaborate ceremonies and rituals that were to be performed in order to atone for the sins of the people. The annual Day of Atonement, on which the high priest would enter the holy of holies in the temple and offer a sacrifice to God on behalf of the people of Israel, is a prime example of ceremonial law. The ceremonial law was designed to point Israel to the Messiah and was, thus, abrogated with the advent of Christ. Similarly, the civil law was Israel's application of the moral law to its civil society. The requirement of restitution in the form of an "eye for eye, tooth for tooth, hand for hand, foot for foot" (Exod 21:24) is a prime example of the civil aspect of the Mosaic law. This aspect of the Mosaic law was intrinsically linked to Israel and the land of Canaan and was, thus, applicable only to the Jewish nation and was abrogated with the destruction of Jerusalem in 70 AD. However, I do recognize the argument, made by theonomists, that the civil law ought to serve as a type of instructional case law for every other state institution as it seeks to interpret and apply God's moral law to its society, but my aim is not to discuss the merits of theonomy. Rather, my aim is to discuss the moral law in relation to Jesus' teaching. The reader ought to pursue further study of theonomy and reach his own conclusions. The purpose here, though, is to contrast the perpetual nature of the moral law with the limited nature of the civil law and the ceremonial law.

The ceremonial and civil law were interpretations and applications of the moral law for a particular people at a particular time within the Mosaic economy. The moral law, however, has always served to reflect the perfect and immutable character of God. For this reason, the moral law is what God has required of all people at all times—including today. There is now a pertinent question that must be asked—namely, what is contained within the moral law? In other words, what does the moral law require of all people at all times?

The Moral Law Summarized in the Decalogue

That the perpetual moral law of God is summarized in the Decalogue, or the Ten Commandments, is seen in Matthew 19. Someone approached Jesus, asking what he must do to inherit eternal life. Jesus responded, saying, "If you wish to enter into life, keep the commandments" (Matt 19:17b). The commandments referred to are clearly those of the Decalogue. This is seen in that Jesus went on to quote five of the commandments in the next two verses. Something similar is seen in 1 John 5:3, which says, "For this is the love of God, that we keep His commandments; and His commandments are not burdensome." This echoes John 14:15, where Christ said, "If you love Me, you will keep My commandments." Once more, Christ summarized the Mosaic law in Matthew 22:37–40 by quoting a summary of the first table of the Decalogue from Deuteronomy 6:5 and a summary of the second table from Leviticus 19:18. The first table contains those commandments pertaining to man's worship of and interaction with God. The second table contains those commandments pertaining to civil interaction or interaction between men. As for the first table, Christ said that it "is the greatest and foremost commandment"

(Matt 22:38) to "love the LORD your God with all your heart, and with all your soul, and with all your mind" (Matt 22:37; Deut 6:5). Concerning the second table, Christ said that it is like the first, and it is to "love your neighbor as yourself" (Matt 22:39; Lev 19:18). Concerning both tables, Christ said that the whole of the Mosaic law depended on these two commandments (viz., Matt 22:40). If the entire Mosaic law was built on these two commands that summarize the Decalogue, it is safe to conclude that the Decalogue outlines the perpetual moral law of God.

Before continuing on with the discussion of the Decalogue, it is important to note that what follows concerning the moral law is not exhaustive. Rather, it should merely serve as an introduction to the moral law for the missionary as he begins to organize his teaching. God's moral law deserves a lifetime of meditation and study (viz., Ps 119:48). The following discourse on the Decalogue is designed only to excite the missionary's mind and point him in the right direction for further study. Also to be noted is that the Decalogue explicitly deals with outward behavior, but it implicitly deals with inward thought and intention. Since God knows the inward thoughts of man (viz., 1 Chr 28:9; Ps 94:11; Matt 9:4, 12:25), it is essential to conclude that God is not only concerned with outward behavior but also with hidden thoughts and intentions. Though the following discourse deals with the outward behaviors commanded and forbidden in the Decalogue, it does so while taking into account the Sermon on the Mount, which clearly includes hidden sins like lust and inappropriate anger in the prohibitions put forth in the Decalogue. With that said, let us now turn to the moral law as outlined in Exodus 20:1–17.

First Commandment

"I am the LORD your God, who brought you out of the land of Egypt, out of the house of slavery. You shall have no other gods before Me" (Exod 20:2–3). Whether the first sentence is seen as part of the commandment or an introduction to and basis for the entire Decalogue is immaterial, for whichever way it is seen does not change the meaning of the commandments. Whether an introduction to the whole or part of the first commandment, God's statement of who he is undergirds the necessity of obeying that which he commands. Because of who God is, man is to have no other gods before the God of Moses. This is the first commandment, and it requires not only that God be exalted above all else but that his glory not be diminished or obscured by ascribing to anything else that which must be ascribed to God alone. Calvin argues that since "we cannot have God without embracing everything which belongs to him, the prohibition against having strange gods means, that nothing which belongs to him is to be transferred to any other. The duties which we owe to God are innumerable, but they seem to admit of being not improperly reduced to four heads: adoration . . . trust, invocation, thanksgiving."[1] Therefore, ascribing adoration, trust, and thanksgiving to anything other than God and making supplication to anything other than God would be in direct disobedience to the first commandment. Furthermore, failing to ascribe the proper adoration, trust, and thanksgiving to God and failing to make proper supplication to God would be in direct disobedience to the first commandment.

Regarding adoration, there are many things that appear worth adoring to the human eye, but the issue at hand concerns to what the adoration is ascribed. Due to the very fact that it is the handiwork of God, creation is adorable, but it is not to be adored apart from its reflection of God. Proper adoration of God includes adoration of his works, but adoration of such works becomes sin when those works are credited to an entity other than God. An example of this is found in Herod's demise recorded in Acts 12:22–23. Though God has made man's mouth and gives eloquence to whom he wishes (viz., Exod 4:11), Herod delivered an address to the people and ascribed his speaking ability to himself. "The people kept crying out, 'The voice of a god and not of a man!' And immediately an angel of the Lord struck him because he did not give God the glory, and he was eaten by worms and died" (Acts 12:22–23). Herod possessed an adorable eloquence in speech but failed to adore such eloquence as a reflection of God.

As for trust, this is one's confident resting in God while waiting for the inevitable fulfillment of his promises. For one to trust God, he must believe that everything God says is true and that God's character is immutable. When one refuses to trust God, he openly declares that God is either a liar or is simply unable to remain faithful to that which he has promised. Both cases constitute a blasphemous rejection of God. Though it seems logically astute to trust an omniscient and omnipotent

---

1. Calvin, *Institutes of the Christian Religion*, 242.

God, mankind has been plagued with a distrust of God and an inclination to trust in things other than him. This is clearly seen at the fall in the garden of Eden. The serpent convinced Eve that God was not worthy of her trust, so she transferred her trust from God's words to those of the serpent (viz., Gen 3:4–6). By her actions and by those of her husband, Adam and Eve declared God to be a liar, and such distrust of God has continued throughout history.

Rebuking those who trusted in their own righteousness, Christ told the parable of the Pharisee and the tax collector in Luke 18:9–14. In the parable, the Pharisee boasted publicly before God and men of his own righteous acts, supposing that such boasting would render him justified. The tax collector, some distance away, beat his chest and cried out to God for mercy. Jesus said, "I tell you, this man went to his house justified rather than the other; for everyone who exalts himself will be humbled, but he who humbles himself will be exalted" (Luke 18:14). To trust in anything other than God or to trust in that that which is not bestowed by God is to have other gods before him.

As for thanksgiving, this is the act of ascribing to God all the blessings that flow from him. James says, "Every good thing given and every perfect gift is from above, coming down from the Father of lights, with whom there is no variation or shifting shadow" (Jas 1:17). God is to be thanked for every good thing given, ranging from each breath of life (viz., Job 12:10) to salvation and eternal life (viz., John 1:9). To thank anything else for that which God bestows is to have other gods before him.

Concerning invocation, this is the act of asking God for that which is needed. In so doing, God is recognized as the giver of that which is needed. When other entities are asked for such things, those entities take God's place and rob him of his glory. Furthermore, the simple failure to make supplication to God ignores God's rightful place as the giver of all things and obscures the glory that is due to him.

To have no other gods before the God who met Moses on Mount Sinai is to adore him and his works alone. It is to trust in him alone for the fulfillment of his promises, not looking anywhere for help other than heaven's throne room. It is to thank God alone for the innumerable blessings that mankind has received, and it is to ask from God for that which is needed.

The Great Enterprise from a Reformed Perspective

Second Commandment

"You shall not make for yourself an idol, or any likeness of what is in heaven above or on the earth beneath or in the water under the earth. You shall not worship them or serve them" (Exod 20:4–5a). This second commandment is similar to the first in that it forbids man to worship any entity other than God, but it differs in its explicit command to not fashion any image. Any image conceived by man to represent God is by definition false, because God is infinite, and the human mind and that which it conceives are finite. Therefore, no image can accurately represent God, and such an image will dull man's mind by obscuring his vision of the endless perfection of God.

Also of importance in this commandment is that there appear to be two things that man is not to make for himself. He is to not make an idol or any likeness. Forbidding the fashioning of any likeness of what is in heaven above, on the earth beneath, or in the water under the earth is a more particular command than that of not making an idol; but if the prohibition were against the making of physical images only, it would have been sufficient to forbid only the fashioning of physical images. However, God saw fit to outlaw the making of all idols, both physical images as well as images conceived in the mind.

The reason physical images were explicitly banned was surely due to Israel's inclination to make such images. Below the same mountain where the Decalogue was delivered, the Israelites later grew weary of waiting for Moses to come down and decided to "make a god who [would] go before" them (Exod 32:1). They gathered together their gold, and Aaron fashioned it and made it into a molten calf. While this behavior was repeated throughout Israel's history, this does not mean the second commandment is to be restricted only to physical images. This is seen clearly in Jesus' response to the crowds in John 6:26–40. He had just fed five thousand people, and they came looking for him the next day. Jesus initially rebuked them by saying that they only sought him because they had eaten "of the loaves and were filled" (John 6:26). He implied that they were no longer full and simply came looking for more bread. In their minds, the Son of God was someone who could make bread out of nothing and give them daily food to eat. They had fashioned an image in their own minds of the Son of God, and their image was false. To them, God was merely a giver of bread, and their vision of his endless perfection was obscured by the false image they had fashioned.

The second commandment not only forbids making and worshiping physical images but also forbids worshiping any concept of God that does not accurately reflect what he has revealed of himself. The reality is that every individual's concept of God is lacking, but God has determined to reveal some of his infinitely perfect character through his works of creation and the Bible. Authentic worship of God and obedience to the second commandment are only possible when thoughts of God are conceived based solely on that which God has revealed of himself. Anything else constitutes idolatry.

Also of interest in Exodus 20:5–6 is God's promise of vengeance on the children of those committing iniquity, while showing lovingkindness to those who keep his commandments. The immediate context is the second commandment, so these words should stand as a stern warning to those who make idols that God will visit their iniquity upon their children to the third and fourth generations. Men do not act alone in this world. The consequences they bring on themselves extend to those for whom they are responsible. While visiting iniquity on the third and fourth generations, God also shows lovingkindness to thousands of those who keep his commandments. This is a declaration of both the justice and the grace of God. He brings iniquity on the third and fourth generations but shows lovingkindness to thousands. This is a stalwart revelation of God's character right in the middle of the Decalogue's summary of the moral law.

Third Commandment

"You shall not take the name of the LORD your God in vain, for the LORD will not leave him unpunished who takes His name in vain" (Exod 20:7). Of utmost importance in interpreting this third commandment is to observe what God's name actually is. Though God's name appears earlier than Moses' encounter with the burning bush, God told Moses in Exodus 6:3 that he did not make himself known by his name to Abraham, Isaac, and Jacob. This statement not only served to solidify God's relationship with Moses but also underlined the significance of God's having revealed his name to Moses at the burning bush. In Exodus 3:13, Moses specifically asked for God's name. God's response was quite magnificent. He said, "I AM WHO I AM" (Exod 3:14). God's name is a declaration of who he is—that he exists in and of himself. No other entity can claim self-existence, for everything else had a beginning. God, on the other hand, never had a beginning. He simply is. God's name reveals him as the preeminent, self-existent one who had no beginning and who will have no end. God's name displays his divinity. Therefore, to trample God's name underfoot is to trample God underfoot. This is why his name is not to be taken in vain.

In order to not take his name in vain, God must be extolled and venerated out of deep reverence through all thoughts, words, and deeds. Any thought of God, word concerning God, or deed done to God must be undertaken with utmost reverence, exalting his excellence and greatness. This requirement pertains not only to the name of God but also to his words and works, because thinking, speaking, and acting in such a way that degrades God's words and works also degrades his name. In sum, man is to offer the reverence due God's name by continually extolling his excellence and greatness and by refusing to drag his name into obscurity with superfluous thoughts, words, and deeds pertaining to God.

The practice of taking an oath is surely to be governed by this commandment as well. According to Calvin, "An oath, then, is calling God to witness that what we say is true."[2] To take an oath while at the same time refraining from using God's name in vain, one must ensure the oath meets two requirements. The oath must first be true. To call God to witness something that is untrue is to call God a liar and openly invite his punishment. While those hearing the oath may not be able to discern the falsity of the matter, God certainly is able to do so, and he will not leave unpunished one who takes such an oath. Second, the oath must not be superfluous. As Jesus said in Matthew 5:37, man is to let his yes be yes and his no be no. Similarly, James says, "But above all, my brethren, do not swear, either by heaven or by earth or with any other oath; but your yes is to be yes, and your no, no, so that you may not fall under judgment" (Jas 5:12). This does not imply that oaths are banned altogether. If this were so, Paul certainly would not have called God as his witness in Romans 1:9. Rather, this simply means that oaths are not to be taken lightly or enacted in unnecessary circumstances.

---

2. Ibid., 246.

Fourth Commandment

"Remember the sabbath day, to keep it holy. Six days you shall labor and do all your work, but the seventh day is a sabbath of the LORD your God" (Exod 20:8–9). There is some disagreement as to the perpetual nature of this law and the manner in which it is to be observed. Regardless, the end of this commandment appears to be meditation on the kingdom of God. The Sabbath was a day of rest in which work was to be refrained from and the Lord remembered. According to Exodus 31:13, the Sabbath was to be a sign that revealed God as the one who sanctifies. Working for six days and resting on the seventh was a sign or a type of the toil with the flesh that mankind endures in this life and of the rest he will enjoy from such toil in the eternal state. The command to keep the Sabbath, therefore, is a command to meditate on the rest from sin in the eternal state that is secured by God who sanctifies. As such, the perpetuity of this commandment includes at least a determined time for meditation on the kingdom of God through the preaching of God's word and the administration of the sacraments. One must remember that the Sabbath was made for man, not man for the Sabbath, and that the Son of Man is Lord of the Sabbath (viz., Mark 2:27–28). Therefore, any Sabbath practice must serve man's sanctification, and the gathering of God's people for the preaching of God's word and the observance of the sacraments serves man's sanctification in a more than sufficient manner.

Fifth Commandment

"Honor your father and your mother, that your days may be prolonged in the land which the LORD your God gives you" (Exod 20:12). To honor one's father and mother is to recognize, through respect and obedience, the place God has given them. Paul echoes this in Ephesians 6:1, saying, "Children, obey your parents in the Lord, for this is right." As his creations, all humans belong to God, but parents act as stewards in God's place in raising their children in the discipline and instruction of God (viz., Eph 6:4). Therefore, to honor and obey one's parents is to honor and obey God, for parents act as representatives of God to their children. When children fail to recognize their parents' place as God's authoritative representatives, they fail to honor God. This is why the commandment carries with it a promise. Honoring God through honoring one's parents brings long life on earth (viz., Eph 6:3). However, only God determines that which constitutes long life on earth, as some are cut down in their youth while other rebels make it to old age. After all, what complaint could an obedient child render when he is hurried into the next life?

All of this, of course, assumes that the parents being honored and obeyed are in the Lord. Paul makes this explicitly clear in Ephesians 6:1. Children are to obey their parents in the Lord. When parents demand anything that obscures God's glory, children are not to obey them. Parents are to be obeyed only insofar as obedience to them will retain God's favor upon such children. When children do obey and honor parents who obscure the glory of God, the parents' iniquity is visited upon the third and fourth generations. This, however, is not necessary, for even children are responsible for their own actions and must render due worship to God, even though their parents fail to do so.

Sixth Commandment

"You shall not murder" (Exod 20:13). This sixth commandment not only forbids murder but also reveals the abominable nature of it. If murder were not detestable in God's sight, it would not be necessary to refrain from committing it. This means that the commandment is twofold. First, man shall not commit murder. Second, man must actively work to protect himself, his family, and his neighbor from suffering the abominable act of murder. It is not enough to simply keep from spilling blood, for the thing that is abominable to God must also be prevented.

This means that in order to fulfill this commandment, man must look after the physical well-being of himself, his family, and his neighbor. This is particularly important for the missionary, as he may find himself living in a hostile environment. No saint is to ever allow murder to take place when he has the capacity to prevent it, even when such prevention requires the use of deadly force. The sixth commandment requires that every saint go to whatever length that is attainable and necessary to protect family and neighbor. Standing idly by while harm befalls another is unacceptable.

This is due to the fact that man was created in the image of God. Therefore, destroying the image of God is equal in severity to destroying God. If a man would not stand by while watching harm befall God, he must not stand by while watching harm befall those made in God's image. The upholding of God's name is far more important than the life of any man seeking to cause harm. It matters not whether such a man will descend directly to hell. What matters most is giving due reverence to God.

Seventh Commandment

"You shall not commit adultery" (Exod 20:14). The meaning of this seventh commandment can only be seen in the context of the meaning of marriage. The marriage covenant is a sign designed to exemplify the union between Christ and the church (viz., Eph 5:32). Just as man was created in the image of God, so was marriage created in the image of Christ and the church. Just as destroying a man is akin to destroying God, so defiling the covenant of marriage is a defilement of the union between Christ and the church. Within the sign of marriage, the husband is representative of Christ, and the wife is representative of the church (viz., Eph 5:23–24). If a man is unfaithful to his wife, he openly declares Christ to be unfaithful and unworthy of the church's faith and trust. Such an act constitutes blasphemy. If a woman is unfaithful to her husband, she openly declares Christ to be unworthy of the church's love and devotion. This act also constitutes blasphemy. The commandment to not commit adultery is a command to always treat the covenant union of marriage with sanctity and reverence as a type or a representation of Christ's union with the church. To approach, conceive of, or participate in the marriage union in any other way would be unfitting to the seventh commandment.

Eighth Commandment

"You shall not steal" (Exod 20:15). Given that injustice is an abomination to God, this eighth commandment requires that whatever is due a man must be rendered. Certainly, a man's property is due him and, therefore, must not be taken from him. Conversely, whatever is owed must be paid. This includes payment of capital, respect, love, obedience, and anything else that may be due. Furthermore, man is not only to refrain from stealing but is to ensure that he, his family, and his neighbor are not stolen from. Man is to conduct his business in an honest and reputable fashion, while at the same time ensuring, to the best of his ability, that the property of others is not plundered.

Ninth Commandment

"You shall not bear false witness against your neighbor" (Exod 20:16). Because God is truth, he requires that men act truthfully towards each other. This means that man is not to slander his neighbor publicly or privately and is to seek the preservation of his neighbor's name and reputation. Neither in the judicial court nor in civil matters is a man to speak falsely or deceitfully regarding his neighbor; and when his neighbor is spoken of in such a way, he must bear true witness to the contrary.

Tenth Commandment

"You shall not covet your neighbor's house; you shall not covet your neighbor's wife or his male servant or his female servant or his ox or his donkey or anything that belongs to your neighbor" (Exod 20:17). With only a cursory reading of this tenth commandment, it may seem somewhat redundant given the previous four commandments. With murder, adultery, theft, and false witness already forbidden, why is it necessary to explicitly outlaw coveting the house of one's neighbor? Is this not already contained in the previous commandments? On the contrary, the tenth commandment is distinct from the others in that it forbids something altogether different.

The distinction is that the previous commandments deal with deeds, thoughts, and words. The tenth commandment, however, deals with covetousness or desire. For this reason, the tenth commandment serves as the greatest indictment on the human race; for even the most debauched men can, at times, regulate their deeds, thoughts, and words. Desire, however, wells up from man's innermost being. While deeds, thoughts, and words are prompted by the will, the will itself is prompted by desire. No man chooses what his desires are. A man's desires are simply a reflection of his natural state. This commandment, therefore, requires man's natural state to be free of the evil desire for his neighbor's home, wife, and property. While it may be theoretically possible in deed, thought, and word not to murder, commit adultery, steal, or bear false witness, every son of Adam is born with evil desires welling up out of his heart (viz., Gen 6:5). For the natural man, there is no way to escape breaking the tenth commandment.

For the regenerate man, however, he is not left to suffer continually at the hand of his flesh. While still carrying the flesh with him, he also has a new nature that wars with the flesh and provides pure and wholesome desires. For the regenerate man, then, the tenth commandment adjures him to be prompted by and act upon the desires of his new nature, while seeking to slay the desires of the old nature.

As the regenerate man acts upon the desires of his new nature, he is indeed able to live in obedience to God's moral law. In fact, the regenerate man enjoys living in obedience to God's moral law and finds it not the least burdensome when acting in accordance with the desires of the spirit. The moral law, as outlined in the Decalogue, not only reveals numerous aspects of God's character but also informs his people of the way in which they ought to live. God's people do not have to drift about wondering what is expected of them. God has graciously made it quite clear, and it is the job of the missionary to teach these things to those who respond in faith to his preaching.

Christ's Teaching Concerning Himself

As the person of Christ is central to the gospel, some of this has already been touched on in the chapter regarding the missionary's preaching. Similar to the previous section concerning the moral law, this section should also be seen as introductory and not exhaustive. The world itself would not be able to contain in writing everything that Jesus did and taught (viz., John 21:25), and an exhaustive exposition of everything recorded about him in Scripture would fill libraries. There are such libraries in existence, and the missionary should seek to benefit from them. This section, however, seeks to outline Christ's essential teachings concerning himself in two ways. This section will, first, examine the name by which Christ most often referred to himself and will, second, consider Christ's teaching in John 3:1–16.

The Great Enterprise from a Reformed Perspective

The Son of Man

Within the Gospels, Jesus is referred to as the "Son of Man" a total of eighty-three times. All but three of these instances appear within a quotation in which Jesus spoke about himself. One exception is in Mark 8:31, which summarizes Christ's words, saying, "And He began to teach them that the Son of Man must suffer many things and be rejected by the elders and the chief priests and the scribes, and be killed, and after three days rise again." The other two exceptions are in John 12:34, where the people questioned Jesus regarding the use of the phrase, saying, "How can You say, 'The Son of Man must be lifted up'? Who is this Son of Man?" Therefore, every reference to Christ as the "Son of Man" either came from his own mouth or from those questioning why he referred to himself as the "Son of Man." The pertinent question for the purposes of this section must now be asked. What does Jesus' self-identification as the "Son of Man" teach us?

To some, it seems rather peculiar that the Son of God almost always referred to himself as the "Son of Man" and virtually never as the "Son of God." This is particularly true given that Numbers 23:19 states that God is neither a man nor a son of man. If Jesus had wanted to demonstrate his deity, why did he not choose a divine name? Referring to himself as the "Son of Man" only served to confuse the people, as opposed to clearly declaring his place within the Trinity, or at least this is what some have been prone to think. In reality, Jesus' reference to himself as the "Son of Man" did not confuse people but only exposed their ignorance. Jesus specifically chose this name in order to show his place in the Godhead; but ignorance of accurate Old Testament doctrine prevented, and still prevents, people from seeing it. Jesus used this particular name in the exact same way he used the phrase, "My God, My God, why have You forsaken Me?" on the cross (Matt 27:46; Mark 15:34). This phrase is from Psalm 22, which includes the prophecy of the Messiah's hands and feet being pierced (viz., Ps 22:16). Anyone who heard Jesus speak those words should have known that he was claiming, based upon Psalm 22, to be the Messiah. Similarly, anyone who heard Jesus refer to himself as the "Son of Man" should have known that he was claiming to be the Messiah, based upon Daniel 7:13–14.

In the first year of King Belshazzar, king of Babylon, Daniel had a dream and wrote it down (viz., Dan 7:1). In the dream, Daniel saw the

Ancient of Days sitting on his throne, which was ablaze with flames and had burning fire for wheels. There was a river of fire flowing out from before him, and myriads upon myriads were standing before him. A court was convened, and books were opened (viz., Dan 7:9–10). Then, the beast was slain, and Daniel kept looking (viz., Dan 7:11–13). "And behold, with the clouds of heaven One like a Son of Man was coming, And He came up to the Ancient of Days And was presented before Him. And to Him was given dominion, Glory and a kingdom, That all the peoples, nations and men of every language Might serve Him" (Dan 7:13–14). This is a clear reference to the second person of the Trinity, who appears like a son of man but is indeed God incarnate and to whom belong dominion, glory, and a kingdom that will not pass away or be destroyed. Jesus' relentless reference to himself as the "Son of Man" was an explicit claim that he is indeed the one presented to the Ancient of Days in Daniel 7:13. The people should never have had to ask, "Who is this Son of Man?" in John 12:34; and those sitting under the teaching of any elder, including the missionary elder, must never have to wonder who the Son of Man is. The nations must be taught to observe Jesus' place within the Trinity as both fully God and fully man, the Son of Man who was coming with the clouds and came up to the Ancient of Days and was presented before him.

John 3:1–16

We now turn to the doctrines presented in John 3:1–16. This passage is chosen because it contains the basic yet essential teaching regarding Christ's substitutionary sacrifice on the cross, his completed work of atonement, and the Holy Spirit's role in enabling the believer to both see and embrace the cross. Also included in this passage is a reference to Christ's posterity, which are "sons of God through faith in Christ Jesus" (Gal 3:26), meaning, that the imputation of Christ's righteousness to his posterity (viz., Gal 3:24) is implicitly included in John 3:1–16.

We will consider these doctrines in the order in which they appear in the text, beginning with the role of the Holy Spirit. Responding to Nicodemus, Jesus said that no one is able to see the kingdom of God unless he is born again (viz., v. 3). Confused, Nicodemus inquired as to how this was possible (viz., v. 4). Jesus then reiterated his statement, saying that one must be born of the Spirit in order to enter into the kingdom of God;

for that which is born of flesh is flesh, and that which is born of Spirit is spirit (viz., v. 5–6). Jesus then went on to explain that the Spirit goes wherever he wants and does whatever he wants (viz., v. 8), clearly intimating that the Spirit regenerates whomever he desires. The summary, therefore, is that in order to see the spiritual kingdom of God, one must be born of, or regenerated by, the Spirit. The flesh is unable to see the kingdom of God and is, therefore, unable to see and embrace the wisdom of the cross. Regeneration by the Holy Spirit is the necessary precursor to seeing and knowing Jesus, and it is impossible to have faith in something that is not known. For Christ to be the object of faith, he must be seen. For him to be seen, the one seeing him must have previously been reborn. Therefore, it is impossible for someone to enter the kingdom of God unless he has been born of the Spirit (viz., v. 5).

Next is the reference to Christ's posterity, which is included in the teaching on regeneration but must be made note of by itself. The reference is in the sixth verse, where Jesus said that the flesh begets flesh and that the Spirit begets spirit. This reveals the way in which someone becomes a child of God and is in turn blessed with the promises of the Abrahamic covenant that were promised to Abraham's seed (viz., Gal 3:16). The physical posterity of Abraham is not included in the promise. If this had been the case, Ishmael and Esau would have been included; but the promise was made to the seed, which is Christ. Therefore, inheritance of the promise is based not upon the Mosaic law or physical descent from Abraham but rather upon union with Christ through faith. Those who belong to Christ through faith are Abraham's descendants and heirs according to promise (viz., Gal 3:29). Through his righteous act on the cross, they are counted righteous in Christ (viz., Rom 5:18) and are made eligible for the promise of eternal life. The imputation of Christ's righteousness is one of his essential teachings; for it is not enough for one, in order to obtain a right standing before God, to merely be cleansed of iniquity. One must also fulfill the law perfectly, which Christ has done on behalf of his posterity—those begotten by the Spirit.

What follows in the next four verses is Jesus' rebuke of Nicodemus for being so ignorant. He then shifted his focus, saying that no one has ascended into heaven but he who descended from heaven—the Son of Man (viz., v. 13). What Jesus said next is absolutely crucial to understanding his work on the cross. He referenced the story of the serpent in the wilderness, which is found in Numbers 21. This incident took place as the people of Israel grew weary and began to speak against God and Moses. God then sent poisonous snakes into the camp of Israel that began to bite and kill the people. This led the people to ask for deliverance, and God designed a cure for those bitten by the serpents. Moses was instructed to make a fiery serpent and set it on a pole so that whoever was bitten could look at it and not die (viz., Num 21:4–9). This is what Christ referenced when he said, "As Moses lifted up the serpent in the wilderness, even so must the Son of Man be lifted up; so that whoever believes will in Him have eternal life" (John 3:14–15). In the same way that Moses lifted up the serpent, Christ was to be lifted up on the cross, which means that if one were to look upon Christ crucified, it would have the same effect as if one were to look upon the serpent in the wilderness. Those who look upon Christ crucified will not die but rather will find eternal life in Christ. Made possible by the miracle of regeneration, gazing upon the substitutionary sacrifice of Christ on the cross causes faith that results in eternal life. Christ had to be lifted up so that he could be seen by those with eyes to see and so that he would be the object of their faith and hope for eternal life.

What Jesus said next is one of the most magnificent truths ever told, but it is sadly one of the most misunderstood. A grievous error has infiltrated the modern church, leading saints to somehow believe that God's overwhelming compassion for the entire human race caused him to sacrifice his only begotten Son on the cross for the sake of all of humanity. The belief is that God loved the world *so much* that he gave his only begotten Son for the sake of anyone who chooses to believe. This, however, is not what Jesus said. He said, "For *in this way* God loved the world, that He gave His only begotten Son so that whoever believes in Him shall not perish but have eternal life" (John 3:16; author's translation). There are two points that are important to notice here. First, the description of God's love is not a reference to the amount of love but rather to the manner in which it was expressed. God did not love the world *so much*. He loved it *in a particular way*. The New American Standard Bible (NASB) translates John 3:16 as, "For God so loved the world . . . " This is the same grammatical structure as John 3:14, which says, "As Moses lifted up the serpent in the wilderness, even so must the Son of Man be lifted up," meaning, that the way in which the Son of Man was to be lifted up was the same way in which the serpent in the wilderness was lifted up. In John 3:16, Jesus did not say that God loved the world a certain amount. He said that God loved the world in a certain way—namely, that he gave his only Son so that whoever believes in him will have eternal life. The way in which God has loved the world is by putting Christ Jesus forward as a propitiation in order to demonstrate his righteousness (viz., Rom 3:24–25). This act was the effectual atonement for all the sins of all those who would believe in Christ through the regenerating work of the Holy Spirit. The iniquity of those united to Christ through faith has been forgiven. The work is finished; and for them, the wrath of God has been exhausted.

Conclusion

These are the kinds of things the missionary must teach to those who respond in faith to his preaching. Christ must be preeminent, and nothing that he taught and commanded is to be ignored or marginalized. The life of the church and the continued spread of the gospel are dependent upon the commandments of Christ being effectively and clearly promulgated in every place where the gospel takes root. No elder has the right to overlook any of the teachings of Christ, thus robbing his people of what Christ himself deemed necessary. While the unfortunate reality within much of Christendom is that many, if not most, of Jesus' teachings have already been jettisoned, the missionary must not follow the same path but instead labor arduously in his teaching to ensure that the church receives the whole counsel of God's word.

A missionary who actually conducts his ministry this way may find less success than those who only teach doctrines palatable to the heathen nations. This, however, should not dissuade him, for the missionary's success is not determined by how many individuals he can dupe into believing a false gospel but rather is determined by obedience to God, who gave the instruction to teach the nations to obey all that Jesus commanded. The missionary who remains true to this instruction, even though few from the nations adhere to his teaching, is to be honored by the church, while the missionary who deceives the multitudes with inaccurate half-truths ought to be rebuked and instructed back into orthodoxy. While even the most faithful elders and missionaries lack perfection, the church must not allow lethargy to hinder its effort to retain orthodoxy. The missionary must teach the nations to obey *everything* that Christ has commanded.

nine

The Missionary's Shepherding

THIS CHAPTER CONSIDERS THE missionary's ongoing responsibilities within the churches that he establishes. The seventh chapter addressed the initial content of the missionary's preaching. The eighth chapter addressed the content of the missionary's subsequent teaching. This chapter addresses the continuing and essential responsibilities of the missionary to the congregation that has gathered around his preaching and teaching. By "continuing essential responsibilities," I mean those responsibilities that must be regularly executed, such as the establishment of the Lord's Day service, the exercising of the means of grace, judging the between doctrinal disputes, and the implementing of church discipline when necessary. Furthermore, the missionary is responsible for leaving the congregation in the hands of capable elders in the event he moves on to another field. While this chapter is not exhaustive of the missionary's role as a shepherd, its content establishes an excellent place to start that protects the sheep and outlines a simple plan for the missionary to be successful in caring for God's people.

The Lord's Day Service

Hinted at in the previous chapter in the discussion on the Decalogue, the doctrine of the Lord's Day teaches that Sunday is a day that ought to be used for God's people to gather for corporate worship, the observance of the sacraments, and the preaching of God's word. This practice is seen as a fulfillment of the moral aspect of the fourth commandment, which is to remember the Sabbath. As stated in the previous chapter, the end of this law is meditation on the kingdom of God. The setting aside of one day every week to meet with God and his people in order to worship him and receive his word, therefore, fulfills the requirement to remember the Sabbath. The practice of designating this day as Sunday began due to the simple fact that it was on a Sunday that the Lord Jesus rose from the dead. Furthermore, some argue that Sunday of each week was the only day in which Jesus appeared to the disciples during the forty days between his resurrection and ascension. Regardless, that the Lord rose on a Sunday is reason enough for his people to meet on Sundays. However, it is not the day that is important but rather the meditation on the kingdom of God. There are practical reasons to meet on Sunday, not mystical reasons. The focus must remain on corporate worship, the observance of the sacraments, and the preaching of God's word.

At this point, it is necessary to mention another teaching concerning the remembrance of the Sabbath. There are those who teach that the moral aspect of the Sabbath law forbids work on Sunday. Sabbatarians, as they are called, assert that Sunday is a perpetual day of rest that must be observed. Sunday must be devoted completely to meditation on the kingdom of God. Similar to the teaching of the Lord's Day, this teaching includes the gathering together of God's people for corporate worship, the observance of the sacraments, and the preaching of God's word as a fulfillment of the command to meditate on the kingdom of God. Contrary to the teaching of the Lord's Day, this teaching forbids any work on Sunday aside from the two exceptions made by Christ. These exceptions are found in Matthew 12:1–13. Demonstrating that the Son of Man is lord of the Sabbath and that the Sabbath was made for man, Jesus and his disciples plucked heads of grain and ate as they passed through the field, and Jesus healed a man in the synagogue. According to Sabbatarians, the two exceptions made here are acts of necessity and acts of mercy. Anything that does not constitute an act of necessity, mercy, or meditation on the kingdom of God is, therefore, forbidden.

The point of this section is not to deal with the differences in these teachings but rather to highlight the main point of each. The end of the fourth commandment for both Sabbatarians and those who follow the teaching of the Lord's Day is that God's people must come together in order to meditate on the kingdom of God through corporate worship, the observance of the sacraments, and the preaching of God's word. That is the point of this section. The missionary must establish the practice of bringing together those who have responded in faith to his preaching for corporate worship and observance of the means of grace.

Means of Grace

Before discussing the various means of grace, it is important to give a definition to this phrase. The Reformed doctrine of the means of grace varies significantly from that of the Roman Catholic Church. According to Roman teaching, grace in the form of forgiveness is actually dispensed to the recipient through the means of grace. All the sacraments of the Catholic Church actually distribute grace through their formal observance. The sacraments, therefore, are the means by which grace is received. The Reformed view of the means of grace is that the sacraments convey grace as opposed to distribute grace, which means that the Reformed sacraments of baptism and communion, along with the preaching of God's word, demonstrate the grace of God so that it can be seen. Grace is bestowed and distributed by God through faith, which is itself a gift from God (viz., Eph 2:8). The means of grace, therefore, act as a sign or a luminary in pointing the saints to the grace of God on the cross. The distinction between the Reformed teaching and that of Rome is critical for the missionary to understand, for some have jettisoned the doctrine of the means of grace altogether in an effort to flee from the Roman deviation from orthodoxy. This reaction, however, is itself a deviation from orthodoxy; for grace is to be conveyed and demonstrated through baptism, communion, and the preaching of God's word.

Baptism

As stated in the previous chapter, it is not the aim of this book to engage in the debate between pedobaptism and credobaptism. Rather, the aim of this book is to outline the essential teachings of the Bible regarding the church and her missionaries' role in the Great Enterprise. As such, baptism must now be addressed but only insofar as it is deemed essential for the missionary to consider. Now, I realize that there are those on both sides of the debate who will argue that I am ignoring issues they consider essential. Indeed, this is true. I am ignoring aspects of the debate that must, at some point, be studied, and I adjure the missionary to study the various doctrines of baptism earnestly as he progresses. The aim herein, however, is to introduce both sides and demonstrate that there is room for both within orthodoxy.

Both views of baptism are fairly straightforward and have sufficient biblical evidence. What the two views have in common is that all new converts to Christianity are to receive the physical sign of baptism as acceptance into God's visible covenant people. In both views, baptism is a sign of Christ's death and resurrection and of the believer's death to sin and his rising again and walking in newness of life (viz., Rom 6:4), and those who respond to the gospel in faith are to repent and be baptized (viz., Acts 2:38). In conveying or demonstrating the resurrection of Jesus Christ (viz., 1 Pet 3:21–22), baptism illuminates the grace of God. Where the two views differ is that one extends the physical sign of baptism to those under the covenant headship of a believer, while the other restricts the physical sign of baptism to those who publicly profess faith in Jesus Christ.

As for the former, pedobaptists argue based on Colossians 2:11–12 that baptism is the sign of entrance into God's visible people under the new covenant and has abrogated the sign of circumcision that served as the physical sign of entrance into God's visible people under the old covenant. As the promises and the sign of the old covenant were for Abraham and his descendants, so the promises and the sign of the new covenant are for the believer and his descendants. Furthermore, pedobaptists argue that God has always dealt and continues to deal with humanity in a covenantal or representative way. Adam acted as the covenant head or representative of all his posterity in the garden of Eden. Christ acted as the covenant head or representative of his posterity in his life, death, and resurrection. Similarly, heads of households have acted and continue to act as covenant heads or representatives of their households. This is why the unbelieving spouse is sanctified by the believing spouse and why their children are rendered holy (viz. 1 Cor 7:14). Paul's statement to the Corinthians only makes sense if God deals with families covenantally based upon the status of the covenant head. As such, God deals with dependent children based upon the status their covenant head—their father. If the covenant head is qualified for entrance into God's visible people, his dependent children are also qualified based upon his status. Therefore, dependent children of

The Missionary's Shepherding

believers are to be given the physical sign of baptism and accepted into the church.

As for the latter, credobaptists argue that every time baptism is administered to a specific individual in the New Testament, it is administered to a believing individual. There are examples, such as the jailer in Acts 16, of entire families being baptized. Credobaptists argue, however, that the entire family could have believed and that such instances do not prove the practice of pedobaptism. Credobaptists further argue based on Romans 6:4 and Colossians 2:11–13 that baptism is expressly administered to those who have experienced regeneration. If baptism is the circumcision of Christ, then God has made the recipient of baptism alive, having forgiven all his trespasses. Paul says it this way, "When you were dead in your transgressions and the uncircumcision of your flesh, He made you alive together with Him, having forgiven us all our transgressions" (Col 2:13). Paul seems to be teaching that baptism is the outward sign of the inward regeneration of the Holy Spirit. Some credobaptists, such as A. W. Pink, further argue that baptism itself is not the sign of entrance into God's visible covenant people but rather is only an outward representation of the inward sign—namely, the gift of the Holy Spirit experienced through regeneration.[1] This argument comes from Ephesians 1:13–14, where Paul says, "In Him, you also, after listening to the message of truth, the gospel of your salvation—having also believed, you were sealed in Him with the Holy Spirit of promise, who is given as a pledge of our inheritance, with a view to the redemption of God's own possession, to the praise of His glory." According to Pink and other credobaptists, believers are sealed with the Holy Spirit through regeneration as a pledge or a sign of God's redemption. This, they argue, is the sign and seal of the new covenant spoken of in Jeremiah 31:31, and baptism is simply the visible representation of what has already taken place inwardly. Because repentance and faith are the evidence of regeneration, only those who have repented and professed faith in Jesus Christ are to be given the outward sign of baptism.

As one can see, there is biblical evidence for both views, and there are great theological minds on both sides. Pedobaptists can claim fellowship with the likes of Calvin and Edwards, while credobaptists gain credence from the likes of John Gill and Pink. The debate will surely rage on until Christ returns. However, one thing is certain. The biblical text

---

1. Pink, *The Divine Covenants*, 53.

is want of explicit teachings and examples regarding the doctrines of baptism. Both pedobaptists and credobaptists reach their conclusions by inference and logical deduction. There is no passage that states explicitly that baptism is to be administered to the children of believers, and there is no passage that states explicitly that baptism is reserved exclusively for those exhibiting evidence of regeneration. Jesus never explicitly taught on baptism under the new covenant, and the apostles seemed to pay little attention to the issue. Therefore, it would behoove the modern church to give the issue similar attention. Based upon what is stated above regarding pedobaptism, there is room for such a doctrine within orthodoxy. Based upon what is said above regarding credobaptism, there is room for such a doctrine within orthodoxy. Therefore, the existence of both views ought to be accepted, and decisions regarding baptism ought to be left up to individual households and their respective covenant heads.

This is critical for the missionary. Whether a pedobaptist or a credobaptist, he will inevitably run into the head of a household within his congregation who uncovers the opposite view within the pages of Scripture. It is impossible to avoid this issue, and the missionary must decide beforehand whether or not he will allow it to be divisive. The missionary must, for the sake of unity, allow variations in doctrine and practice so long as such variations do not constitute heresy. Hopefully, the missionary can see room within orthodoxy for both views regarding baptism. If not, I beg him on behalf of God's people to continue his study and treat those of an opposing view with grace and respect.

Before moving on to the next section, the essential teaching regarding baptism for the missionary must be made explicit. Whether a pedobaptist or a credobaptist, the missionary must baptize those who respond in faith to his preaching. Peter demonstrated this in Acts 2:37–38. Peter preached a convicting sermon, and the people "were pierced to the heart, and said to Peter and the rest of the apostles, 'Brethren, what shall we do?' Peter said to them, 'Repent, and each of you be baptized in the name of Jesus Christ for the forgiveness of your sins; and you will receive the gift of the Holy Spirit.'" After they responded in faith, Peter immediately instructed the people to be baptized. The missionary must act in the same manner by baptizing those who respond in faith to his preaching, bringing them into God's visible covenant people—the church.

The Missionary's Shepherding

Communion or the Lord's Supper

Instituted by Christ at the Last Supper, communion, or the Lord's Supper, is the practice of remembering the blood of the new covenant. Jesus broke bread and gave it to his disciples, saying, "Take, eat; this is My body" (Matt 26:26b). He then took a cup and gave thanks and said, "Drink from it, all of you; for this is My blood of the covenant, which is poured out for many for forgiveness of sins" (Matt 26:27b–28). Paul elaborates in 1 Corinthians 11:26, saying, "For as often as you eat this bread and drink the cup, you proclaim the Lord's death until He comes." Therefore, communion is the act of breaking bread and drinking wine by believers in remembrance of Christ and his broken body and shed blood on the cross.

Grace is conveyed through communion because it visibly demonstrates the sacrifice of Christ on the cross and proclaims the Lord's death. For this reason, it ought to be done as often as believers gather for corporate worship. Paul seems to assume the practice of weekly communion within the Corinthian church, saying, "Therefore when you meet together, it is not to eat the Lord's Supper" (1Cor 11:20). He says this in the middle of his rebuke of their approach to communion, but he assumes that they approached the Lord's Supper every time they met together. However, there is no scripturally required frequency. Many churches within orthodoxy have practiced communion biweekly or monthly. The aim of this section, however, is not to address the arguments pertaining to the frequency of communion but rather to plead with the missionary to convey grace to his sheep through communion as often as is beneficial.

Three brief points must be made before moving on to the discussion on the preaching of God's word. The first point is the critical difference between the Roman doctrine of transubstantiation and the Reformed practice of the Lord's Supper. As with all the Roman sacraments, grace is literally distributed to the recipient during the Mass. Transubstantiation literally means that the substance is transformed. In this context, the bread and the wine are literally transformed into flesh and blood. According to Roman teaching, the bread and the wine literally become the broken body and shed blood of Christ. The sacrifice of Christ on the cross is not only remembered weekly but also conducted weekly. In consuming Christ's actual body and blood, the recipient is given grace and will live forever (viz., John 6:51). This practice has nothing in common with the Reformed practice of the Lord's Supper, other than the presence of bread and wine. According to Reformed teaching, the bread and wine are merely bread and wine. They do not change into anything or acquire any other substance. The elements are only symbols that represent the body and blood of Christ. Nothing mystical happens to the believer who consumes the elements, but he is edified in that he has remembered the blood of the new covenant.

The second point has to do with that of the elements themselves. Jesus used bread and wine. The bread was probably unleavened, and the juice from the fruit of the vine was certainly fermented. Therefore, the use of unleavened bread and fermented wine is certainly acceptable. However, it is important to note concerning the bread that there is no specific mention of the lack of leaven. Because of this, many have concluded that the requirement is merely that bread be used and that the presence of leaven is immaterial. Given that the design of communion is that the broken body of Christ be remembered, the stipulation concerning the bread should only be that it is able to represent the broken body of Jesus. Concerning the cup, the same argument can be made. The cup Jesus used was certainly full of fermented wine. As many in the Corinthian church were getting drunk, their practice was obviously to use wine (viz., 1 Cor 11:21). Therefore, the practice of using wine for communion is certainly acceptable. As with the bread, though, the design is that the cup represent the shed blood of Christ. The stipulation concerning this element, therefore, ought to be that the content of the cup be of the fruit of the vine and accurately represent the blood of Christ.

The third point may very well be the most significant, as it deals with the serious nature of the Lord's Supper. Referenced earlier was Paul's rebuke of the Corinthians, but it must now be further expounded. In 1 Corinthians 11:27, Paul says, "Therefore whoever eats the bread or drinks the cup of the Lord in an unworthy manner, shall be guilty of the body and the blood of the Lord." The severity of this statement must not pass the reader by. Whoever takes communion in an unworthy manner is guilty of crucifying Jesus Christ. For this reason, Paul goes on to say that each man must examine himself and that some among the Corinthian church were actually dying as a result of participating in the Lord's Supper when they ought to have refrained (viz., 1 Cor 11:28–30). Clearly, the Lord's Supper is to be guarded and administered only to those known to be in good standing with God and men. There is no open invitation to communion. The Lord's Supper is reserved for known believers who have examined themselves as evidenced by their good standing within the congregation. These requirements, however, are not foolproof. An unbeliever or a believer with hidden sin may still sneak up to the table, but it is the responsibility of the missionary to administer communion to those who appear to be qualified for it and to deny communion when the evidence demonstrates disqualification. If an unqualified individual lies and sneaks up to the table, judgment will be on his head. If an unqualified individual comes to the table unchallenged, judgment will be on his head as well as that of the missionary.

The Preaching of God's Word

As the sacraments of baptism and communion visibly convey grace, so the preaching of God's word audibly conveys grace. Paul makes it clear in all of his epistles that grace comes through the word of God. Without exception, Paul begins his letters by saying, in some form, "Grace to you." Without exception, Paul ends all of his letters by saying, in some form, "Grace be with you." As the recipients of his letters began reading the inspired word of God, grace started coming to them. By the time they finished reading the inspired word of God, grace was with them. Paul's implicit point is that grace is conveyed to the hearer of God's word. This is crucial for every congregation, but it is of utmost importance for the missionary who works among peoples with limited access to the Scriptures or with low literacy rates. God's design is that grace be conveyed to his people through the written and inspired words of Scripture. However, some are unable to read or live without access to the Bible. For these saints, grace must be conveyed to them through preaching. For those with access to the Scriptures, personal study and mediation are essential, but these must still be coupled with corporate preaching. In receiving the preached word of God, saints' capacities for beholding the glory of God are enlarged more than if the word of God is merely studied in private.

For this reason, the missionary is to make preaching central to the Lord's Day service. As an elder, he has been given the authority and responsibility to teach and prescribe doctrine. While the sacraments convey very specific aspects of God's grace, preaching is to convey the whole counsel of God's will—to the praise of the glory of the grace of God (viz., Eph 1:6). As shown in the previous two chapters, a whole lifetime will not exhaust the entire counsel of God's will as revealed in the Scriptures, but it remains the missionary's responsibility to faithfully exposit God's word to the best of his ability whenever his sheep are gathered together for corporate worship.

Judging between Doctrinal Disputes

An often overlooked role of the elder is his responsibility and authority to judge between doctrinal disputes. By "doctrinal disputes," I mean those instances within the congregation where there is disagreement over or questions about what the Bible prescribes and/or allows. This could range from issues regarding the deity of Christ and the order of salvation to the acceptability of a saint's potential marriage partner. Similar to Moses, the elder is to judge between parties and render judgment on questions not because he has some secretive and mystical access to God but rather because he is aware of God's ordinances. Moses said in Exodus 18:16, "When they have a dispute, it comes to me, and I judge between a man and his neighbor and make known the statutes of God and His laws." Moses acted as judge because he was aware of the statutes of God and his laws. Similarly, the elders of today must be able to prescribe the statutes of God and have final authority in the church to give answers and judge between parties.

Exercising Church Discipline

Church discipline is another role of the eldership that is often overlooked. Most modern saints have never seen church discipline actually take place; and if they have seen it, it is often done in a perverted fashion. Christ prescribed the process of church discipline quite clearly in Matthew 18:15–20. The passage is a familiar one, but the actions prescribed rarely take place. If a brother sins, the victim is to show him his fault in private. If the brother repents by confessing and seeking restitution, he has been won over, and the victim is to forgive him. If the brother refuses, witnesses can be brought to him in order to confirm his sinful action. If the brother still refuses, the matter is to be brought to the church. Because the authority of the church rests with the elders, they are to render a public judgment on the basis of two or three witnesses as to whether or not the brother's action has broken the statutes of God and his law. If the brother listens and repents by confessing and seeking restitution, he has been won over and is to be offered forgiveness. If the brother still refuses, he is to be removed from the communion table and treated as an unbeliever.

Why this process causes so much consternation in the modern church is a mystery. In 1 Corinthians 5, Paul certainly has no problem excommunicating the brother who had his father's wife. Similarly, modern elders ought not have any hesitation in disciplining those who deny the God and Father of the Lord Jesus Chris by their licentious behavior or rejection of essential biblical doctrine. With 26 percent of evangelicals in America having been divorced as of 2008,[2] roughly an eighth of all evangelicals should have faced discipline and possible excommunication for either committing adultery or breaking the marriage oath. An eighth of all evangelicals in America should have, at some time, faced some kind of discipline due to only one issue. One can only imagine how many more issues there are that should have led to the discipline of multitudes, yet the church carries on for the most part as if discipline was for another time.

When church discipline does take place, it too often happens behind closed doors in an effort to insulate the people from the process. Trying to look out for the best interests of the congregation, elders too often seek to deal privately with public matters of sin in the church. Public matters are to be dealt with publicly; and issues brought to the elders are, by definition, public. Dealing with such matters privately robs the congregation of the opportunity to learn to fear the Lord God (viz., Deut 21:21) and weakens the discipline that is designed to save the one who has sinned (viz., 1 Cor 5:5). To treat discipline this way is unbecoming of an elder. Church discipline must be executed with diligence and accuracy to the word of God, with the primary objective being obedience to God's ordinances.

This is particularly true for the missionary, who will inevitably face licentious behavior and rejection of essential biblical doctrine as he organizes young sheep into a functioning congregation. If such behavior and rejection of truth are tolerated at the beginning, there is little to no hope of the church flourishing and the name of God being honored among that people. For the sake of the praise of the glory of the grace of God among the nations and the well-being of those who respond in

---

2. "New Marriage and Divorce Statistics Released," Barna Group, para. 5.

faith to his preaching, the missionary must diligently exercise biblical church discipline.

Appointing Elders

The importance of this final section cannot be stressed enough. The missionary is responsible for the spiritual well-being of those who respond in faith to his preaching. This is clear from Hebrews 13. The author instructs believers to obey their "leaders and submit to them" (Heb 13:17a). Who these leaders are is defined earlier, when the author says, "Remember those who led you, who spoke the word of God to you; and considering the result of their conduct, imitate their faith" (Heb 13:7). So, believers are to obey and submit to their leaders, and their leaders are the ones who spoke the word of God to them. This scenario is seen clearly in the missionary context. The missionary proclaims the gospel. Individuals respond in faith and are to imitate the faith of the missionary as they submit to and obey his teaching. The author of Hebrews explicitly highlights the missionary's responsibility for the well-being of those who respond in faith to his preaching in Hebrews 13:17, saying, "Obey your leaders and submit to them, for they keep watch over your souls as those who will give an account. Let them do this with joy and not with grief, for this would be unprofitable for you." The missionary is charged with keeping watch over the souls of his sheep, and he will give an account for the manner in which he has kept watch.

This means that the missionary is biblically required to keep watch over his sheep until other shepherds are appointed, to whom authority of and responsibility for the church are transferred. The missionary must remain with the church that forms as a result of his preaching and must not move on to another field at least until he is able to appoint and ordain elders who are able to shepherd the flock in his place. The missionary has not successfully completed his mission if he prematurely abandons his sheep and, thus, orphans them to the world. The shepherding work of the missionary is long and complex, and he must see it to fruition. After being mistreated and stoned in Iconium, Lystra, Pisidian Antioch, and Derbe in Acts 14, Paul and Barnabas went back to strengthen the souls of the disciples and encourage them in their faith, and they did not leave until they had appointed elders for them in every church (viz., Acts 14:22–23). Paul and Barnabas understood their responsibility and entrusted the souls of the disciples to capable elders. The modern missionary must do the same.

It is important here to briefly outline the biblical requirements for eldership, as the missionary must recognize these things in those whom he appoints and ordains as elders. Paul gives the following requirements for eldership in 1 Timothy 3:1–7. An elder must be above reproach, the husband of one wife, temperate, prudent, respectable, hospitable, able to teach, not a drunkard, not violent, gentle, peaceable, and without the love of money. He must manage his household well, not be a new convert, and have a good reputation among outsiders. Furthermore, Paul lists the following requirements in Titus 1:6–9. An elder must be above reproach, the husband of one wife with obedient and believing children, not self-willed or quick tempered, not addicted to wine, not violent or fond of sordid gain, hospitable, loving good, sensible, just, devout, self-controlled, holding fast the faithful word in accordance with the apostles' teaching, and able to both exhort sound doctrine and refute those who contradict. These requirements are fairly straightforward and must be observed by the missionary in anyone he appoints and ordains to the eldership.

Conversely, extra-biblical stipulations must not be used in the process of identifying and appointing elders. God did not see fit to include any other requirements, and the missionary ought not either. An elder does not have to accept a particular view of baptism or have a particular number of children. He does not have to accept a particular view of creation or earn a certain amount of money. An elder does not have to have a particular degree or come from a particular family. All of these issues are superfluous and must not be taken into account by the missionary as he appoints elders. What must be taken into account are the biblical requirements listed by Paul. If a man meets those requirements, then he is eligible for eldership, and the missionary may consider ordaining him for the office of elder and transferring the authority of and responsibility for the church to him.

Final Thoughts

The missionary's shepherding, as outlined in this chapter, is rarely given consideration by modern missionaries. This is probably due to the fact that most missionaries are robbed of the biblical authority to act in these

The Great Enterprise from a Reformed Perspective

capacities. Churches send out unqualified missionaries to feed hungry people and share the gospel with their neighbors, while neglecting to consider the ramifications of sending missionaries in that fashion. Every saint is qualified to feed hungry people and give an account for the hope that he has. Missionary activity, however, is much more than a saint recounting his experience and sharing what he knows of the gospel. The church must not continue to treat missionary activity in this way. Rather, the church must identify, ordain, and send qualified missionaries to preach the gospel among the heathen nations, teach them to obey all that Christ has commanded, and watch over the souls of their flocks as those who will give an account for the way in which they have shepherded. When this happens, the nations will exult in the exaltation of Jesus Christ; and the honor, worship, and glory that is due God will be rendered. The best is indeed yet to come when the glory of the Son shines on all his elect gathered around his throne. That day is coming. God's Great Enterprise will indeed reach its end, and it would behoove the church to align herself with God's expectations now, for it is time for judgment to begin with the household of God (viz., 1 Pet 4:17). There is yet time. We may still succeed. The church may still shine as a city on a hill throughout the world, but it will not happen without hard work and diligence. We must embrace our responsibilities and act in accordance with what God has revealed in Scripture. This is the only acceptable path forward.

ten

The Missionary and Suffering

THIS FINAL CHAPTER IS devoted to the issue of suffering in the life of the missionary. All saints encounter some kind of suffering in their lifetime. It is an inevitable reality that everyone faces. Everyone loses loved ones, and most encounter some kind of physical suffering as earthly bodies decay through illness and disease. There are countless other ways in which saints are made to suffer in this world. Given the geographical areas and sometimes hostile communities in which missionaries find themselves, they are particularly prone to experiencing suffering on a level to which other saints are not necessarily exposed. While it behooves every saint to develop a doctrine of suffering in order to remain faithful when suffering comes, it is essential for the missionary to understand God's design behind suffering in order to have any success in the mission field. The aim of this chapter, therefore, is to expose the purpose of suffering by addressing the three reasons why suffering exists.

Suffering Exists for Discipline

Ann Judson was the first wife Adoniram Judson, the first missionary to preach the gospel to the people of Burma in the early 1800s. After ministering in the Burman land for a short time, she wrote a letter to her parents in New England that detailed their first encounter with miserable suffering, saying, "Our little Roger Williams, our only little darling boy, was three days ago laid in the silent grave. Eight months we enjoyed the precious little gift, in which time he had so completely entwined himself around his parents' hearts that his existence seemed necessary to their

The Great Enterprise from a Reformed Perspective

own."[1] The rest of the letter detailed the sweet joy the Judsons experienced through little Roger and the acute pain they endured at his departure. In dealing with the grief, she lamented to her mother that while some mothers at home may lose their firstborn, they still remained in a Christian country surrounded by friends and relatives who could help soothe such anguish, while she and her husband remained solitary and alone in a pagan land. To lose an eight-month-old firstborn son in a heathen nation, separated from the church, friends, and family must have been nearly unbearable.

Indeed, it would have been unbearable without an accurate doctrine of suffering. While the Judsons may have been ill-prepared in some ways, they were not wanting of God's purposes for suffering. Mrs. Judson made this clear in her letter to her parents, saying, "But God has taught us by affliction, what we would not learn by mercies—that our hearts are his exclusive property, and whatever rival intrudes, he will tear it away."[2] The Judsons had become so infatuated with their darling little boy that their hearts were prone to wander from the glory of God and delight merely in the joy of their son. For this reason, according to Mrs. Judson, God took little Roger from them so that their hearts could once again be exclusively God's. This may be hard for some moderns to accept, but it is indeed what she believed. In order to discipline the Judsons' hearts back to him, God killed their firstborn son.

To give clarification to the nature of discipline is now of extreme importance, for at this point some may conclude that God punished the child along with the Judsons for their sin. This, however, could not be further from the truth. Discipline is not punishment. For the believer, the wrath of God has been satisfied. God's wrath was exhausted on Jesus Christ for the sins of Christ's posterity. Therefore, there is no more wrath or punishment for those united to Christ through faith. This point must be made explicitly clear. God does not punish believers, for he has already punished Christ in their place. No saint should ever fall into the trap of thinking that he is being punished for something he has done, and little Roger William Judson was not punished for his parents' sin. Rather, Roger was a means of discipline for his parents, and discipline must never be confused with punishment.

1. Stuart, *Lives of the Three Mrs. Judsons*, 35.
2. Ibid.

"Discipline" means to train or instruct or correct. While the wrath of God has been satisfied, these things remain necessary in the life of the believer. All saints need continuous training and instruction and correction. These things constitute the process of sanctification, and at times God sees fit to use suffering as a means of discipline. It is important to note that God may discipline a saint when he has done something wrong, which would be for correction, or when he is simply lacking the correct behavior, which would be for training. When God disciplines a saint, it does not necessarily mean the saint has sinned. While it could come as a result of sin, discipline may also simply be a means of maturation. While Mrs. Judson claimed that their affliction came due to their delighting in their son more than in God, the aim of discipline is always instruction. They suffered the loss of their son in order that their hearts would be instructed back to God. This is the case with all the various forms of discipline.

Paul makes this clear in 2 Corinthians 1:8–9, saying, "For we do not want you to be unaware, brethren, of our affliction which came to us in Asia, that we were burdened excessively, beyond our strength, so that we despaired even of life; indeed, we had the sentence of death within ourselves so that we would not trust in ourselves, but in God who raises the dead." Paul says that he and Timothy were afflicted beyond their strength, so much so that they believed they were going to die. Paul then gives the reason for the affliction, namely, that they would not trust in themselves but rather in God. Two things are important to notice. First, Paul implies that God is the one doing the afflicting. This is seen in the reason for the affliction. They were afflicted so that they would trust in God. No one other than God would have this aim. While the affliction may have come at the hands of Satan or other opponents to the gospel, it ultimately came at the hand of God. Second, Paul does not say whether he and Timothy had actually trusted in themselves or not. All he says is that God afflicted them so that they would not trust in themselves but instead in God. The conclusion, therefore, ought to be that the same means of discipline can be used for both correction and training. Had they trusted in themselves, that would have been sin, and affliction to the point of death would have come in order to reveal their sin and direct them back to God. Were they just in need of a deeper trust in God, the same affliction to the point of death would have come in order to train them to trust in God as opposed to trusting in themselves.

The Great Enterprise from a Reformed Perspective

The point is that all saints are in need of discipline, and God will often use affliction and suffering as a means of implementing such discipline. When this happens, it behooves the saint to sit submissively under the rod and seek the end for which such affliction has come, not questioning the wisdom of the Almighty. The words of Job provide a wise example. "Though He slay me, I will hope in Him" (Job 13:15a). Though at times God afflicts his people with terrible circumstances, they must continue to hope in him. This is particularly true for the missionary, for discipline in the form of suffering is inevitable. For Mr. Judson, the death of his firstborn son was only the beginning. By 1827, eleven years after the death of little Roger, Judson had endured nearly two years in a torturous Burmese prison and the subsequent death of his wife and their second child, Maria. Judson wrote on April 26, 1827, saying, "My sweet little Maria lies by the side of her fond mother . . . The work of death went forward, after the usual process, excruciating to a parent's feelings, she ceased to breathe on the 24th, at 3 o'clock P.M., aged 2 years and 3 months . . . The next morning we made her last bed, under the hope tree, in a small enclosure which surrounds her mother's lonely grave."[3] The agony of the loss was nearly too much for Judson. Over the next two years, he spiraled into a deep spiritual depression, living in isolation in a hut in the jungle. Having dug his own grave and waiting to die, he wrote another letter, saying, "God is to me the Great Unknown. I believe in him, but I find him not."[4] Similar to the experience of Paul, Judson's affliction had brought him to the point of death; and even though everything he thought he knew of God had been destroyed, his belief and trust in God remained.

This should serve as incredible encouragement to the missionary. Judson lost his wife and two young children, which drove him to a level of despair unknown to most of God's people. In the depths of his depression, he dug his own grave and admitted he was failing in his search for God, yet his faith remained. Through it all, Judson believed God. When discipline through suffering comes, the missionary must believe God. The missionary must believe that God is who he says he is and that God is and will remain faithful to his promises.

---

3. Ibid, 106.
4. Anderson, *To the Golden Shore*, 391.

Suffering Exists in Order to Fill Up What Is Lacking in Christ's Afflictions

In Colossians 1:24, Paul says, "Now I rejoice in my sufferings for your sake, and in my flesh I do my share on behalf of His body, which is the church, in filling up what is lacking in Christ's afflictions." Here, Paul explicitly links his own sufferings with that which is lacking in Christ's afflictions. Before we address the two things lacking in Christ's afflictions and their relationship to Paul's suffering, let it first be clearly stated that the atoning work of Christ on the cross is in no way deficient or incomplete. On the contrary, the atoning work of Christ is totally sufficient and completely finished. The whole work of atonement has been completed for those united to Christ through faith. Paul did not do anything to finish the work and neither do saints today. Atonement is wholly a work of God that has been accomplished once for all who believe (viz., 1 Pet 3:18).

Concerning the two things actually lacking in Christ's afflictions, both are implied in Colossians 1:24. As for the first, Piper has accurately observed an eye-opening link between the grammatical structure in Colossians 1:24 and in Philippians 2:30. These are the only two places in the Greek text where that which is lacking is filled up or completed. In Colossians 1:24, Paul says that he is filling up what is lacking in Christ's afflictions. In Philippians 2:30, Epaphroditus risked his life to complete what was lacking in the Philippian church's service to Paul. The church in Philippi loved Paul and desired to serve him; but what they had lacked, until Epaphroditus brought their gift to Rome, was the opportunity to serve Paul. Their love for Paul was not deficient. They simply lacked the opportunity to express their love for him through service. Piper writes, "Now that's exactly what I think Colossians 1:24 means . . . Paul's self-understanding of his mission is that there is one thing lacking in the sufferings of Jesus. The love offering of Christ is to be presented in person through missionaries to the peoples for whom he died . . . Christ intends for the Great Commission to be a presentation to the nations of the sufferings of his cross through the sufferings of his people."[5] In other words, one thing lacking in Christ's afflictions is the display of those afflictions. Christ was afflicted, suffered, and died on a cross two thousand years ago; but those afflictions are represented or symbolized by the afflictions of Christ's missionaries for the benefit of the nations, from which God's elect

---

5. Piper, *A Holy Ambition*, 116.

will emerge at the preaching of the gospel. No one born after Christ's death has been able to visibly observe Christ's afflictions. However, Christ's afflictions are pointed to and typified by the visible afflictions of God's people. The visible display, therefore, is the first thing lacking in Christ's afflictions.

The second thing is implied in the words, "I do my share on behalf of His body, which is the church" (Col 1:24). There is a profound union that the church shares with her Savior; and Paul references it in Philippians 3:10, saying, "That I may know Him and the power of His resurrection and the fellowship of His sufferings, being conformed to His death." There is such a thing as the fellowship of Christ's sufferings. Through enduring affliction as believers, saints are able to identify with the sufferings of the Lord and commune with him in an intimate way. "Blessed are those who have been persecuted for the sake of righteousness, for theirs is the kingdom of heaven" (Matt 5:10). Sharing in the sufferings of Christ is a down payment of the kingdom of heaven. This may seem odd at first, for how can suffering be a down payment of the kingdom of heaven? Those with spiritual eyes to see and a heart of flesh to feel, however, know that the sweet communion with the Lord that is found in the fellowship of his suffering is indeed the appetizer prior to the main course of the eternal state. Indeed, it has been granted to the church "not only to believe in Him, but also to suffer for His sake" (Phil 1:29b). God has shown favor to the church by allowing her to share in the sufferings of Christ. The fellowship of his sufferings, however, has not yet been completed. There are yet those within the church and those who have yet to be called from among the nations who have more of this fellowship to embrace. This is the other thing lacking in Christ's afflictions, namely, the church's full participation in the fellowship of Christ's sufferings.

In these two ways, Paul filled up what was lacking in Christ's afflictions on behalf of the body. First, his own afflictions served as a visible symbol to the nations of the afflictions of Christ. Second, he did his part to fill up what was lacking in the church's fellowship with Christ through suffering. All saints have various roles to play in this fellowship, and Paul saw his role as a significant one. While Christ's work of atonement is finished, the visible display of his afflictions and the church's participation in the fellowship of Christ's sufferings will continue until he returns. It is absolutely essential for the missionary to understand this. He will suffer in order to visibly demonstrate Christ's afflictions to the nations, and the church that forms as a result of his preaching will participate in the fellowship of Christ's sufferings. There is no room within orthodoxy for the so-called prosperity gospel. "Indeed, all who desire to live godly in Christ Jesus will be persecuted" (2 Tim 3:12). Christian converts in hostile lands will be slaughtered. Missionaries will be thrown into prison. HIV/AIDS will continue to ravage Africa. Families will be torn apart. Babies will continue to die. Droughts will destroy crops, causing widespread famine. Wars will continue to break out. Yet, the gospel does not promise that any of these things will change. Preachers spit in the face of Christ when they tell desperate people that if they will just accept Jesus, their diseases will go away, herds will flourish, crops will multiply, and worldly concerns will vanish. The prosperity gospel is an abomination, and the missionary must fight against it at every turn. He must not allow it to contaminate his own theology, and he must protect his flock from its hellish lies.

Suffering is part of the Christian life. All saints experience it on some level, but the missionary is prone to experience and see the severity of it often. Whether the suffering encountered is correction from an error, training in maturity, a symbol to the nations, or fellowship in Christ's afflictions, the missionary is required to embrace it, still trusting that God is faithful to his promises. Remember, "God causes all things to work together for good to those who love God, to those who are called according to His purpose" (Rom 8:28). God causes all things, even suffering and affliction; and because God is the cause of all things, saints can rest in the promise that all things happen for their good. Though weeping may often last through the night, the shout of joy comes in the morning (viz., Ps 30:5). God is indeed faithful, and he will eventually wipe away every tear (viz., Isa 25:8; Rev 21:4). Until then, let the church and her missionaries know that the High Priest is one who sympathizes with weakness and has been tempted in all things just as are the saints; and "let us draw near with confidence to the throne of grace, so that we may receive mercy and find grace to help in time of need" (Heb 4:16).

The Chief Reason why Suffering Exists

There is yet one final question that must be answered before this chapter is concluded. For, some may accept that God causes all things to work together for the good of his people, but they may still wonder why suffering has to exist at all. In other words, why is it necessary that suffering exist in the world? The answer has been implied throughout the book, but it must now be stated clearly, both to avoid confusion and to provide comfort. Some have tried to answer this question by pinning everything on Adam and claiming that suffering is a result of original sin. While this may be somewhat true, it is still insufficient, for it does not answer the question of why suffering ultimately exists. If suffering exists because of sin, why does sin exist? If sin exists because Adam ate the fruit, why was he allowed to eat the fruit? This questioning process must continue until God's chief design is uncovered.

The chief end for which God created the world was discussed in chapter 1. God's aim or design in all his works is his own glory—namely, the glory of his grace on the cross. God created the universe so that Jesus Christ, the Mediator, could come to the earth as God incarnate, live a perfectly obedient life, suffer the wrath of God on the cross, and rise from the dead, all on behalf of his posterity. All of this has been done "to the praise of the glory of His grace" (Eph 1:6a). God's chief end for creation is that his glory would shine throughout the world through the life, death, and resurrection of Jesus Christ. Suffering is intricately linked to God's design of and purpose for creation. The universe exists so that Christ could suffer on the cross and display the glory of God for the nations to see and worship. Suffering is at the center of God's design, for it was determined beforehand that Christ would suffer. Therefore, it is necessary for suffering to exist in order for Christ to have suffered on the cross. If suffering did not exist in the world, Christ would not have been able to complete his work as the Mediator, and there would be no hope at all of salvation. Suffering must exist, for it is the only way in which God's people can be redeemed.

The wisdom of God's design is not to be questioned. Rather, it is to be embraced. His thoughts and ways are so far beyond those of man (viz., Isa 55:9). Yet, God has been so gracious as to not leave us in the dark, wondering why tears are made to flow in the church like water from an abundant yet bitter spring. He has shown us the design behind our suffering, and it is a magnificent design. We suffer now so that Christ could suffer then on our behalf. This morsel of truth ought to be as sweet as honey on the tongue of God's suffering people. Not only that, Christ has now gone to prepare a place for his people in his Father's house (viz., John 14:3). He first prepared a place of suffering for us in this world, but now he is preparing a wholly different place for us. "And the ransomed of the LORD will return And come with Joyful shouting to Zion, With everlasting joy upon their heads. They will find gladness and joy, And sorrow and sighing will flee away" (Isa 35:10).

This is why "we eagerly wait for a Savior, the Lord Jesus Christ; who will transform the body of our humble state into conformity with the body of His glory, by the exertion of the power that He has even to subject all things to Himself" (Phil 3:20b–21). Suffering must exist in this world in order for the church to have a Savior, but this is not true of the next world. While this world necessarily groans and suffers the pains of childbirth (viz., Rom 8:22), the church ought to "rest in the LORD and wait patiently for Him" (Ps 37:7a). Sharing in the fellowship of Christ's sufferings may be necessary, but it is not perpetual. Endure the afflictions now, but "keep seeking the things above, where Christ is, seated at the right hand of God" (Col 3:1b).

appendix

What Is the End for Which God Created the World?

INHERENT IN THE STUDY of the Great Enterprise is a question. If one is to examine the way in which a thing is the means to an end, the end itself must be known in order to understand the intricacies of the means. In other words, the purpose of a thing must be known in order to appreciate how the thing works. A thing can only be said to be functioning properly if it is achieving its end. If its end is unknown, then it cannot be known if the thing is achieving its end. If it cannot be known if it is achieving its end, then it cannot be said that it is functioning properly. Therefore, the end of a thing must be known in order to comprehend the thing.

This leads to the inherent question. What is the end for which God created the world? If the design of missionary activity within the Great Enterprise as a means to an end is to be examined and known, the end to which it is a means must first be examined and known. Having a means without an end is an impossibility. So, what is God's end for creation? In other words, why did God create the world originally, and why does he sustain it continually and act within it sovereignly?

Notice that there is a presupposition in the question—namely, that God exists and that he sovereignly created and sustains the universe. Presupposed also is that God is infinite, omniscient, and totally self-sufficient in everything, meaning, that he does not need anything that does not come from himself. That the reader accepts these presuppositions is assumed.

Concerning some terms that require further definition, what is meant by "end" in describing the purpose for which God created the

Appendix

world? There are various kinds of ends that fall into the two general categories of "subordinate ends" and "ultimate ends." According to Edwards, "A subordinate end is what an agent aims at, not at all upon its own account, but wholly on the account of a further end, of which it is considered as means."[1] For example, a man drives his car to the pharmacy to purchase medicine. Purchasing the medicine is the end for which the man drives his car to the pharmacy. However, purchasing the medicine is not that at which he aims. Rather, he purchases the medicine on account of his desire to alleviate an illness. The end of purchasing medicine is subordinate to a further end.

"An ultimate end," according to Edwards, "is that which the agent seeks in what he does, for its own sake; what he loves, values, and takes pleasure in on its own account, and not merely as a means to a further end."[2] Concerning the man driving to the pharmacy, alleviating his illness is that at which he aims. He values the alleviation of the illness for its own sake and not merely as a means to something else. So, driving to the pharmacy is a means of attaining the subordinate end of acquiring medicine, and the acquisition of the medicine is a means of attaining the ultimate end of alleviating the illness.

Before we continue, clarification is needed regarding what is not being said about means. Nothing is said regarding the appeal of various means themselves. That means cannot be enjoyable in themselves is not accurate. When the man drives to the pharmacy, he may be driving his new convertible with the top down, and he may find the act of driving to the pharmacy enjoyable. He only drives to the pharmacy to acquire the medicine, yet he may find enjoyment in the means of acquiring the medicine. Similarly, means can be dreadful in and of themselves, carrying no appeal to the agent apart from the end to which they work. If the same man is hiking in the desert and is bitten by a poisonous snake, his trek out of the desert may well be excruciating. Hiking to civilization is the means used to acquire the anti-venom necessary to alleviate the illness. All of this is to say that the end does not necessarily determine the appeal of the means. Means can, in and of themselves, range from enjoyable to dreadful. This is true of means that are not ends in and of themselves, as well as means that are subordinate ends to further ends.

1. Edwards, "A Dissertation Concerning the End," 95.
2. Ibid.

Appendix

Furthermore, nothing is said here as to the nonessential nature of the means. In other words, it should not be assumed that certain means are not essential. On the contrary, means are, by definition, essential to the reaching of the end. If the man does not drive to the pharmacy, he will not reach the end that he seeks. As such, means are equally essential to the ends they serve. A clock is a prime example. The clock maker puts in motion countless mechanisms and wheels, which are never seen from the outside, and this serves the ultimate end of telling time. If so much as one cog or wheel fails, the entire system fails. Therefore, let it be noted that means are just as essential as their ends.

There is yet another type of end that is, by definition, "ultimate" yet still more particular. This third type of end is known as a "chief end." "A chief end is something diverse from an ultimate end; it is most valued, and therefore most sought after by the agent in what he does."[3] The man seeks the ultimate end of alleviating his illness. Such alleviation is ultimate because he values it for its own sake. If nothing else comes of the alleviation, such alleviation still has value. This is not true of the subordinate end of acquiring the medicine. If the medicine does not alleviate the illness, then the acquisition of the medicine no longer has any value. Beyond this, there may still be a chief end for which the man seeks. His illness may prevent him from working, which in turn prevents him from providing for his family. So, he drives to the pharmacy to acquire medicine to alleviate the illness so that he can return to work and provide for his family. There is in this sequence a simple means, a subordinate end, an ultimate end, and a chief end. The chief end is what is meant by "end" in describing the purpose for which God created the world.

As for what is meant by "world" in describing the end for which God created the world, the Greek word referenced is *kosmos*. The English translation is "world," and it carries a meaning of orderly placement. Hebrews 1:2 refers to Jesus as the one "through whom also [God] made the world (*kosmos*)." Acts 17:24 refers to "the God who made the world (*kosmos*) and all things in it." The understanding is that *kosmos* refers to the entire created realm. Therefore, what is meant by "world" is all aspects of the created realm. Included is everything in the physical realm, which is denoted by its being experienced through the five senses, as well as everything in the moral realm. The moral realm is denoted by its being

---

3. Ibid.

experienced by the will or psyche of certain moral agents, namely, human beings. Examples of those things experienced of the moral realm are emotions and intellect. So, the world that God created for a certain end consists of everything that exists within time and space, whether it be a distant galaxy or a person's capacity for reasoning.

Now, the question at hand remains. What is the end for which God created the world? There are two ways to determine the reason for which something was made. The maker of the thing can be consulted either through direct questioning or objective observation, or the result of the thing itself can be observed, thus shedding light on the purpose for which it was made. The former will be the focus of the rest of this essay.

If it is to be known why someone does a thing, he could simply be asked why he does a thing. In some instances, though, the man may not be available for questioning. This is certainly the case with government leaders. If the purpose for which the president of a country implements a particular policy is left wanting, the average citizen is not able to ask the president for the purpose for which the policy is being implemented. The citizen must resort to other means. While the citizen cannot ask the president directly, he can listen to what the president says. He can observe the president's overall goal by acquainting himself with the president's desires and aspirations. If the president implements a tax cut for the purpose of allowing citizens to keep more of their money, he will probably be heard talking about his desire for citizens to be able to keep more of their money.

This same principle is true with regard to the question at hand. God has created the world. As God is totally sovereign, omniscient, and wise, it can be presupposed that he did not create the world by accident. If he did not create the world by accident, then it must be assumed that he created the world purposefully. If he created the world purposefully, then it must be assumed that there is a purpose for which he created the world. If there is a purpose for which he created the world, then it must be assumed that he can be heard speaking of the purpose for which he created the world.

Just as the president's goals and desires can be observed by listening to him, so can God's goals and desires be observed by listening to him. If there is a chief end towards which God works, it can be assumed that God can be heard speaking of this chief end. As God is a revelatory God, meaning, that he reveals himself to his creation, it can safely be assumed that he reveals that which is most dear to him or that at which he chiefly aims. When God speaks of the ends for which he acts, at what is most chiefly aimed? To God's own words is where the focus now shifts.

Why did God create his sons and daughters? Isaiah 43:6–7 says, "Bring My sons from afar And My daughters from the ends of the earth, Everyone who is called by My name, And whom I have created for My glory, Whom I have formed, even whom I have made." God is here quoted by the prophet Isaiah in reference to the redemption of Israel from exile and the final ingathering of God's elect from the ends of the earth. This is an amazing work God has claimed to do, including deliverance from physical troubles like floods and fires and the giving of other peoples as a ransom for the life of his people. The time frame of this work was to cover thousands of years. This is manifestly a great work of God, and he has bestowed the blessing upon the reader of sharing why he would execute such a great work. God redeemed Israel from exile and will finally save all of his elect because he created his people for a purpose. He created them *for his glory*. The glory of God was chiefly aimed at in the redemption of Israel from exile and will be the chief end of the ingathering of his elect from the ends of the earth.

Why did God take for himself Israel as his possession? Jeremiah 13:11 says, "'For as the waistband clings to the waist of a man, so I made the whole household of Israel and the whole household of Judah cling to Me,' declares the LORD, 'that they might be for Me a people, for renown, for praise and for glory.'" God clearly stated that he caused Israel to cling to him that they might be his people. God continued and said that Israel were his people for the sake of renown, praise, and glory. Again, the glory of God was chiefly aimed at in his taking Israel as his possession.

Why did God rescue Israel from Pharaoh in the midst of their forgetfulness and rebellion at the Red Sea? The psalmist says in Psalm 106:7 –8, "Our fathers in Egypt did not understand Your wonders; They did not remember Your abundant kindness, But rebelled by the sea, at the Red Sea. Nevertheless He saved them for the sake of His name, That He might make His power known." God's name was at stake as the Israelites camped between Migdol and the sea. Furthermore, God having acted for the sake of his name served a further end—namely, that he might make his power known. This display of God's power, or his glory, was chiefly aimed at in his saving the Israelites from Pharaoh and splitting the Red Sea.

Appendix

This is further manifest in observing the reason for which Pharaoh pursued the Israelites into the sea. Exodus 14:4 says, "Thus I will harden Pharaoh's heart, and he will chase after them; and I will be honored through Pharaoh and all his army, and the Egyptians will know that I am the LORD." God continued in verse 17, saying, "As for Me, behold, I will harden the hearts of the Egyptians so that they will go in after them; and I will be honored through Pharaoh and all his army, through his chariots and his horsemen." God caused Pharaoh to not only pursue the Israelites into the wilderness but also into the sea; and he did this for a reason, namely, for his own honor. God hardened the heart of Pharaoh, causing him to behave in such a way that resulted in the death of his entire army and the destruction of his chariots. This was to the honor of God and resulted in the nation of Egypt knowing that the Lord is God. The glory of God was chiefly aimed at in the destruction of Pharaoh and his army in the Red Sea.

Why did God spare the Israelites again and again in the wilderness? Ezekiel 20:14 says, "But I acted for the sake of My name, that it should not be profaned in the sight of the nations, before whose sight I had brought them out." In the previous verse, God resolved to pour out his wrath and annihilate Israel due to their rejection of his ordinances. This happened over and over, but God continually acted for the sake of his name in the exercising of grace.

The theme of God acting for the sake of his name runs through the entire book of Ezekiel. Four other times it is explicitly stated that God acted for the sake of his name. "But I acted for the sake of My name" (20:9). "But I withdrew My hand and acted for the sake of My name" (20:22). "Then you will know that I am the LORD when I have dealt with you for My name's sake" (20:44). "It is not for your sake, O house of Israel, that I am about to act, but for My holy name" (36:22). An implicit statement is found in 36:32, "'I am not doing this for your sake,' declares the Lord GOD, 'let it be known to you. Be ashamed and confounded for your ways, O house of Israel!'" Furthermore, some variation of the phrase "Then they will now that I am the LORD" (6:10) is used seventy-four times in Ezekiel. The statement is made repeatedly and emphatically that the result or chief end at which God has always aimed in his actions is that his creation would know that he is the Lord. The glory of God was chiefly aimed at in all of God's works in the book of Ezekiel.

Appendix

Why did God not cast away his people when they rejected him as king and asked for a king like the nations? First Samuel 12:20-22 says, "Do not fear, You have committed all this evil, yet do not turn aside from following the LORD . . . For the LORD will not abandon His people on account of His great name." Here, the Israelites have rejected God as their king. Their wickedness was great in the sight of the Lord. God sent thunder and rain that day, causing the people to greatly fear both the Lord and Samuel (viz., 1 Sam 12:18). Yet, God responded to them with great mercy, not on account of them but rather on account of his holy name. God caused such a thunderstorm that the people were stricken with fear, and God then comforted them with the emphatic statement that he would act only for the sake of his name.

Why did God use his sovereign power to bring back his people from exile after punishing four generations of sin? Isaiah 48:9-11 says, "For the sake of My name I delay My wrath, And for My praise I restrain it for you, In order not to cut you off. Behold, I have refined you, but not as silver; I have tested you in the furnace of affliction. For My own sake, for My own sake, I will act; For how can My name be profaned? And My glory I will not give to another." For the sake of God's name, he delayed his wrath. That God might be praised, he restrained his wrath and tested his people in the furnace of affliction. God acted for his own sake in accord with his jealousy for his own glory so that his name would not be profaned nor his glory given to any other. One cannot escape God's explicit statement that his own glory was what he chiefly aimed at in his actions.

Why did the Son of God come to earth and to his final decisive hour? John 17:1 makes a remarkable proclamation. Christ's hour has come, the hour of his crucifixion. This was not only the hour towards which his ministry had been leading but was also the hour to which all the law and the prophets had pointed. This hour was the reason Christ came to earth. So, what does Scripture say regarding the chief end of this hour? "Father, the hour has come; glorify Your Son, that the Son may glorify You" (John 17:1). All of the law and the prophets and Christ's ministry on earth led to an hour that was designed for the purpose of glorifying the Son of God so that he might glorify the Father. The most significant event in the history of the world, the sacrifice of the Son of God on the cross, was brought about for the purpose of glorifying God.

Why has God called his saints out of darkness and into light? First Peter 2:9 says, "But you are a chosen race, a royal priesthood, a holy nation,

Appendix

a people for God's own possession, so that you may proclaim the excellencies of Him who has called you out of darkness into His marvelous light." The saints of God are a chosen race. God selected them from among all the peoples of the world and set them aside as a royal priesthood and a holy nation. They are a people who are for God's possession, and all of this has been done for one purpose. God has done this so that his saints may declare that God is excellent. The proclamation of the manifold perfection of God, his glory, was chiefly aimed at in God calling his elect out of darkness and into his marvelous light.

Why did Christ instruct his disciples to be shrewd as serpents and innocent as doves (viz., Matt 10:16)? The immediate context is that they were being sent out as sheep in the midst of wolves, but why were they being sent out as sheep in the midst of wolves? "You will even be brought before governors and kings for My sake, as a testimony to them and to the gentiles" (Matt 10:18). The disciples were sent out into the midst of wolves so that they would be brought before governors and kings. They were brought before governors and kings as a testimony to the nations, and all of this was for Christ's sake.

Finally, why will Jesus come again in the great day of consummation? "These will pay the penalty of eternal destruction, away from the presence of the Lord and from the glory of His power, when He comes to be glorified in His saints on that day, and to be marveled at among all who have believed" (2 Thess 1:9–10). The day for which the church longs, the day of the return of the Lord Jesus Christ, is a day designed for Christ to be glorified among his saints and marveled at by all those who believe. The explicit end of the physical return of Christ to earth is that he would be glorified and that his church would marvel at him.

So, it is abundantly clear through these various passages that the end at which God chiefly aims in all his acts from creation to consummation is his own glory. God is jealous for his name and has acted and continues to act in such a way that most prominently displays his glory. The glory of God is the chief end for which God created and sustains the world and continues to act within it sovereignly.

These passages are adequate to confirm that God's end for creation is his glory. However, God has seen fit to go beyond adequacy; so one final passage will be examined, showing clearly God's end in his blessing, choosing, predestining, adopting, redeeming, and forgiving the saints. Let the first recorded act of God in the Bible be examined. Numerous

Appendix

accounts of this act are found in various forms, but Ephesians 1:3–6 shall be looked at specifically. "Blessed be the God and Father of our Lord Jesus Christ, who has blessed us with every spiritual blessing in the heavenly places in Christ, just as He chose us in Him before the foundation of the world, that we would be holy and blameless before Him. In love He predestined us to adoption as sons through Jesus Christ to Himself, according the kind intention of His will, to the praise of the glory of His grace, which He freely bestowed on us in the Beloved." This passage states what God has done, when he did it, and why he did it.

First, let what God has done be considered. Verse 4 tells of God's choosing the saints, and verse 5 tells of God's predestining the saints. Second, when did God do this? Verse 4 tells that this happened before the founding of the world—that is, before Genesis 1:1. According to 2 Timothy 1:9, this may have taken place before anything even was; for the saints were called, or chosen, and given grace in Christ Jesus "from all eternity." Nothing happened before all eternity. Therefore, it is safe to say that God did this act before anything else even existed.

Third, why did God do all of this? Verse 4 tells that the saints were chosen to be holy and blameless before him. Verse 5 tells that they were predestined as sons according to the kind intention of his will, but these answers are not the end. God chose them that they would be blameless, but why did he want the saints to be blameless? God predestined them as sons according to his will, but why did he want to adopt them as sons? Verse 6 gives the ultimate answer. God did all of this ultimately to the praise of the glory of his grace. God has acted from all eternity to bless, choose, predestine, and adopt his saints so that the glory of his grace might be displayed and he might be praised for it, but there is still yet more. Ephesians 1:7–12 says, "In Him we have redemption through His blood, the forgiveness of our trespasses, according to the riches of His grace which He lavished on us . . . In Him also we have obtained an inheritance, having been predestined according to His purpose who works all things after the counsel of His will, to the end that we who were the first to hope in Christ would be to the praise of His glory." The means mentioned here are redemption and forgiveness—both according to that which was purposed in Christ to the end of the praise of his glory. God states explicitly that his chief end is that his glory be seen through his acts and that his saints worship him on account of his seen glory. From beginning to end, God's ultimate goal is to display his glory and for him to be worshiped.

Bibliography

Anderson, Courtney. *To the Golden Shore: The Life of Adoniram Judson*. Grand Rapids: Zondervan, 1956.
Barna Research Group. "New Marriage and Divorce Statistics Released." Barna Group. Accessed February 3, 2012. http://www.barna.org/family-kids-articles/42-new-marriage-and-divorce-statistics-released.
Calvin, John. *Institutes of the Christian Religion*. Translated by Henry Beveridge. Peabody, MA: Hendrickson Publishers, 2009.
Drewery, Mark. *William Carey: A Biography*. Grand Rapids: Zondervan, 1981.
Edwards, Jonathan. "A Dissertation Concerning the End for Which God Created the World." In *The Works of Jonathan Edwards*. Vol. 1, edited by Edward Hickman. Carlisle, PA: The Banner of Truth Trust, 2005.
Joshua Project. "Great Commission Statistics." Joshua Project. Accessed February 21, 2012. http://www.joshuaproject.net/great-commission-statistics.php.
———. "How Many People Groups Are There?" Joshua Project. Accessed February 28, 2012. http://www.joshuaproject.net/how-many-people-groups.php.
———. "What is the 10/40 Window?" Joshua Project. Accessed January 19, 2012. http://www.joshuaproject.net/10-40-window.php.
Lausanne Movement. "About." Lausanne Movement. Accessed January 15, 2012. http://www.lausanne.org/en/about.
MacArthur, John. *Ashamed of the Gospel: When the Church Becomes Like the World*. Wheaton, IL: Crossway Books, 1993.
Newbigin, Lesslie. *The Gospel in a Pluralist Society*. Grand Rapids: Eerdmans, 1989.
Pink, Arthur W. *The Divine Covenants*. Grand Rapids: Baker Book House, 1973.
Piper, John. *A Holy Ambition: To Preach Where Christ Has Not Been Named*. Minneapolis: Desiring God, 2011.
———. *God Is the Gospel: Meditations on God's Love As the Gift of Himself*. Wheaton, IL: Crossway Books, 2005.
———. *Let the Nations Be Glad: The Supremacy of God in Missions*, 2nd ed. Grand Rapids: Baker Academic, 2003.
Stuart, Arabella W. *Lives of the Three Mrs. Judsons*. Gloucester, United Kingdom: Dodo Press, 2009.
U.S. Center for World Mission. "Our History." U.S. Center for World Mission. Accessed January 15, 2012. http://www.uscwm.org/index.php/about/our_history/.
Walker, Deaville F. *William Carey: Missionary Pioneer and Statesman*. Chicago: Moody Press, n.d..

www.ingramcontent.com/pod-product-compliance
Lightning Source LLC
Chambersburg PA
CBHW071857160426
43197CB00013B/2516